CONTEMPORARY INSIGHTS FROM BIBLE CHARACTERS

Paul T. Culbertson

Baker Book House
Grand Rapids, Michigan

ISBN: 0-8010-2350-5
Copyright 1973 by
Beacon Hill Press of Kansas City
Reprinted 1973 by
Baker Book House with the permission of
Beacon Hill Press

Formerly printed under the title

Contemporary Portraits from the Old Testament

Appreciation is expressed to the Macmillan Company for permission granted to quote R. C. Yarbrough's poem from *Triumphant Personality*, and to Hodder and Stoughton for permission to quote G. A. Studdert-Kennedy's poem from *The Unutterable Beauty*.

Quotations from copyrighted versions of the Bible are as follows:

The New Testament in Modern English, © J. B. Phillips, 1958. Used by permission of the Macmillan Co.

The New English Bible, © The Delegates of the Oxford University Press and the Syndics of the Cambridge University Press, 1961.

The Holy Bible, *Revised Standard Version*, copyrighted 1946 and 1952 by the Division of Christian Education of the National Council of Churches. Used by permission.

PHOTOLITHOPRINTED BY CUSHING - MALLOY, INC.
ANN ARBOR, MICHIGAN, UNITED STATES OF AMERICA
1973

CONTENTS

PREFACE

The Old Testament is an unusually rich source of biographical material. A careful and sympathetic study of selected personalities provides much instructive material in the art of successful living.

Each of the personalities whose stories are presented here represents some pertinent contemporary issue or problem in the development of personality or moral character, or some failure or success in creative living. In each instance, a careful, nontechnical summary of biblical material is combined with insights and observations from recent studies of personality, moral character, or human relationships.

Here are some representative topics which are included: understanding the problem of suicide; the relation of perception to psychic energy; combining adaptability with moral strength; building frustration tolerance; applying the sacramental principle to the whole of life; gambling versus calculated risks; resolving conflicting inner motives; meeting the challenge of unrelieved stress; overcoming the shadows of the past; becoming self-actualized persons.

Over half of the persons chosen for this study are not too well known: Ahithophel, Jabez, Bath-sheba, Eliakim, Nebuchadnezzar, Joash, Manasseh, Balaam. Others are "old favorites," presented with, we hope, a new emphasis or approach: Job, Ruth, Esther, Elijah, Esau, Caleb, Daniel.

Someone has said that "those who do not learn from history are doomed to repeat it." The Apostle Paul, speaking of the children of Israel, puts it more hopefully, "Now all these things happened unto them for ensamples: and they were written for our admonition, upon whom the ends of the world are come" (I Cor. 10:11).

Many of the worthies whose lives are cited in these pages were true pioneers of the faith. Like Abraham, they "went out" not knowing whither they were going. Yet by faith they sought for a city whose Builder and Maker is God.

We, too, are pioneers. As Dr. James B. Chapman subtly observed, "We are the true ancients, for we lived in our fathers." But, standing on their shoulders, we should be able to see farther; and, being nearer the goal, we should walk with a steadier gait and a brighter hope.

—PAUL T. CULBERTSON

1

ELIJAH:
When Psychic Energy Runs Low

And he requested for himself that he might die; and said, It is enough; now, O Lord, take away my life; for I am not better than my fathers (I Kings 19:4). These are the words of a great and courageous man who was in the throes of an emotional depression. He had irrationally concluded: "There is nothing to live for; all is lost. What's the use of going on? I might as well be dead."

Elijah's hopeless despair arose in part from a downward swing of his cycloid temperament. It probably wasn't the first time that his feelings had shifted from extreme elation to the depths of depression—nor the last!

Another reason for his depressed state of mind was that his psychic energy was abnormally low. The result was that his perception of himself, his problems, other people, and even the Lord God of Israel, was greatly distorted.

What is psychic energy? Well, like physical energy, it is the force or energy needed to do work. What kind of work? The answer: *psychic* work. This includes such activities as seeing, hearing, understanding, remembering, thinking, deciding, and so on.

At any given moment each of us has a certain amount of pyschic energy. It is derived from physical energy. Consequently, it is closely related to our physical condition. Our psychic energy level falls when we become tired, are hungry, or are suffering from some weakening illness such as the flu or T.B. Conversely, the psychic energy level rises when we are rested, well fed, and in robust health.

Over a period of years the distribution and use of psychic energy explains, in part, the kind of personalities we will have. If the energy is used in developing the *ego*, a person will be a thinker, a scientist, an executive. If it is primarily used in developing the *conscience*, a person will become a moralist, greatly concerned with matters of right and wrong. If the energy is largely used to energize the *biological drives*, a person will be a sensualist.

In the "short run" the distribution of psychic energy determines our moment-by-moment behavior. Such energy "runs" our psychic machinery by which we perceive, think, choose, and act. Since at any given moment we have just so much psychic energy—no more and no less—if it is used for one purpose, we have that much less for any other purpose. This is the basis of an amusing story told about David Starr Jordan, a pioneer president of Stanford University. He was an ichthyologist—an expert on fish. It was said of him that every time he learned the name of a new student he forgot the name of a fish! Psychic energy was shifted from the names of fish to the names of students. True or not, the story illustrates the point that efficiency in behavior is dependent on the skillful and astute use of the available psychic energy at every given moment.

As the psychic energy level rises or falls throughout the day, important changes occur in behavior and experience. This is aptly illustrated in the observations of a small boy lying awake at night:

The apples falling from our tree
  Make such a heavy bump at night,
I always am surprised to see
  They are so little, when it's light.

And all the dark just sings and sings so loud!
  I cannot see at all
How frogs and crickets and such things that make
  The noise can be so small.

Then, my own room looks bigger, too;
  Corners so dark and faraway.
I wonder if things really do
  Grow up at night, and shrink by day.

Yes, that is exactly how it is! And why? Because of the lowered psychic energy level at 3 a.m. and its influence on perception. Problems which appear insignificant in the full light of day may seem to be utterly insoluble and totally overwhelming in the middle of the night.

With these facts about psychic energy and perception in mind, let us return to our account of Elijah and his emotional depression.

Elijah's story is partially recorded in the nineteenth chapter of I Kings. He was one of the most colorful and dramatic characters in the Old Testament. Whatever he did was headline news! His depression was immediately preceded by a dramatic confrontation with the forces of evil and idolatry on Mount Carmel (I Kings 18).

With little or no introduction, Elijah had appeared on the stage of history about three and one-half years earlier. From the outset he showed himself in his characteristic

11

role: boldly challenging the forces of evil as personified in Ahab, the wicked king of Israel; and Jezebel, Ahab's evil-minded, Zidonian wife. Elijah courageously warned Ahab and Jezebel of the coming judgment of God on their personal sin and on Israel's idolatry. The penalty: no rain in the land for three years and six months!

At the conclusion of this devastating drought, Elijah again appeared unannounced. He boldly challenged Ahab and the 450 prophets of Baal to a contest on Mount Carmel. The manifesto was: "Let the God who answers by fire from heaven be God!"

When the Lord God of Israel did answer Elijah's simple, believing prayer by fire from heaven, the prophets of Baal were routed, and Elijah himself took charge of their forthright liquidation!

Elijah then turned to intercessory prayer that rain might come again to the drought-stricken land. Before long the sky was black with rain-laden clouds. Elijah's advice to King Ahab was, "Prepare thy chariot, and get thee down, that the rain stop thee not." So "Ahab rode, and went to Jezreel. And the hand of the Lord was on Elijah; and he girded up his loins, and ran before Ahab to the entrance of Jezreel" (I Kings 18:44-46).

Then came the letdown for Elijah. It was triggered by the wicked, painted Jezebel. It all started when "Ahab told Jezebel all that Elijah had done, and withal how he had slain all the prophets with the sword. Then Jezebel sent a messenger unto Elijah, saying, So let the gods do to me, and more also, if I make not thy life as one of them by tomorrow about this time" (I Kings 19:1-2).

In other words, Jezebel said, "Elijah, you have had it. You will be as dead as the prophets of Baal within 24 hours." Frightened by this threat, Elijah "arose, and went for his life" (I Kings 19:3). So Jezebel had God's valiant prophet on the run! What a demonstration of the power of a wrathful, decisive woman with a diabolical purpose!

So Elijah "took to his heels." Running for his life, he came to Beersheba, on the northern edge of the Negev desert. Here he unwisely left his servant and went a day's journey alone into the wilderness. It was there, sitting down under a broom bush, commonly called a "juniper tree," that he requested of the Lord that he might die.

On Mount Carmel, Elijah had been excited, confident, elated. He reveled in the public contest with the prophets of Baal. He chided them mockingly, and later destroyed them in a burst of religious enthusiasm. After praying successfully for rain, he outran Ahab's royal horses for 17 miles as the lightning flashed, the thunder rolled, and the rain poured. His whole demeanor was that of an unconquerable man of tremendous energy, force, and confidence.

Then came the reaction and letdown. From high elation his emotions took a steep downward swing. As he sat alone under the juniper tree, his attitude was one of defeat, discouragement, depression. Joy was gone. Only gloom and dejection remained.

At this point we can well understand what the Apostle James meant when he wrote that Elijah was a man "subject to like passions as we are" (Jas. 5:17). We too know what it feels like to have an attack of the blues.

It seems obvious that Elijah was physically and psychologically exhausted. He had urged King Ahab to eat and drink (I Kings 18:41) but he probably failed to do so himself. Rest and sleep had been out of the question. There was too much excitement! And it was no small task to liquidate the 450 false prophets in an all-day confrontation. Then his 17-mile, cross-country run ahead of Ahab's royal chariot drained all of his reserve supply of energy.

Now, sitting alone with both his physical and psychic energy at an all-time low, his problems were seen as completely insoluble and overwhelming. His response was, "It is enough; now, O Lord, take away my life" (I Kings 19:4).

Elijah, like you and me, lived in two worlds. There is the *objective* world out there consisting of things, people, and situations as they really are. But there is also the *assumptive* or *perceptive* world—the world *as we perceive it*. In this sense each of us lives in two worlds. And this private, perceptive world in which each of us lives every moment is the true *reality* for you and me.

This is why a person must enter into the perceptive world of another person, to some degree, in order to really communicate with that person. Parents, for example, to communicate with their children, must learn to see through their eyes, hear through their ears, feel through their emotions. We must never forget that the world of reality for every person is his or her perceptive world.

Now, at the very center of a person's perceptive world is his perception of himself—his *self-image*. This is why it is so important for a person to have a realistic, healthy self-image. When Elijah's psychic energy went down, his image of himself was greatly distorted. Imagine one of the greatest of the Old Testament prophets saying, "I am not better than my fathers." And especially so soon after one of the most incredible defeats of idolatry and evil forces ever recorded. He was saying, in effect, "My fathers didn't succeed in eliminating the worship of Baal from Israel. Neither have I. We are all dismal failures."

The importance of a wholesome self-image in producing victorious living is urged upon us by the Apostle Paul in Rom. 12:3: "As your spiritual teacher I give this piece of advice to each one of you. Don't cherish exaggerated ideas of yourself or your importance, but try to have a sane estimate of your capabilities by the light of the faith that God has given to you all" (Phillips).

Of course, it is important to avoid both inferiority and superiority complexes. But many people "sell themselves too short." They underestimate their capabilities.

In the healing processes of counseling there is almost always an improvement of the self-image.

As a person's self-concept improves, there is usually an improvement in human relationships. Those who respect themselves respect others. Those who hate others begin by hating themselves. Only those who healthily love themselves are capable of loving others as they love themselves.

In addition to a distorted self-image, Elijah's low level of pyschic energy led to a distorted view of other loyal and faithful Israelites. In the counseling interview between the Lord and the discouraged prophet one of the Lord's questions was, "What doest thou here?" And Elijah defensively replied, "I have been very jealous for the Lord God of hosts: for the children of Israel have forsaken thy covenant, thrown down thy altars, and slain thy prophets with the sword; and I, even I only, am left; and they seek my life, to take it away" (I Kings 19:10).

In response to the Lord's question, "What are you doing here?" Elijah might well have answered, "I am adding up the results of a total spiritual and personal defeat. And when I add up the number of those who are loyal and faithful to Jehovah, I get a total of one—and *I am that one.*" The Lord's rejoinder was immediate and devastating, "Elijah, your perception and, consequently, your mathematics are all wrong! The total is not one but 'seven thousand.'" And that "seven thousand" probably stood for a much larger, silent majority of those who had never bowed their knees to Baal.

And so it is. When our psychic energy is low, we are likely to have inaccurate perceptions of other people. Many marriages might have been saved if husbands and wives had remembered this. They argued about trivialities when they were so tired that they could not accurately perceive either the problem or each other's motives. It's a wise person who knows when it's time to shut up and go to bed.

Elijah's lowered psychic energy level also greatly influenced his perception of the immediate presence of God. On Mount Carmel, Elijah's psychic energy, as we have seen, was at or near an all-time high. Fire was falling from heaven; God and His prophet were being vindicated; and the false prophets of Baal and Jezebel were in full retreat. And, of course, Elijah was very much aware of the presence and power of God.

Now he was on another mountain—Horeb, "the mount of God." For more than 40 days he had been in the desert alone. Everything was very quiet! Where was God now?

The Lord had already provided His servant with nourishing food and undisturbed rest. His physical and psychic energies were on the mend. Now the Lord would help him with his perception of the divine presence with some nondirective counseling and psychodrama.

Twice the petulant prophet was led to ventilate his feelings of injustice, his resentments against overwhelming forces of evil, and his sense of desertion and loneliness.

Then came the psychodrama: a great and strong wind which broke rocks and rent the mountains, a violent earthquake, and a consuming fire. But the Lord was not in the wind, the earthquake, or the fire. How surprised Elijah must have been!

Then came the "still small voice," and Elijah came to understand that God could be known and heard in the quietness and silence of the desert. *God had been with him all the time.* He had never been really alone!

Lowered psychic energy, distorted perceptions, and emotional depression all tend toward the stopping of responses. Elijah was now ready for action again. So the Lord gave him a new and challenging task.

The prophet could now return to his work with new zest, a clearer perception of himself, of God's sustaining presence, and the support of at least 7,000 other faithful and loyal people.

The Apostle James was right! Elijah was a man very much like you and me. He and we know what it means to become exhausted and depressed. But God knows us, too. And in His dealings with the disheartened prophet we too may discover the way out of every Cave of Giant Despair.

2

NEBUCHADNEZZAR:
Learning Humility
The Hard Way

Nebuchadnezzar was a colorful, Oriental despot. His story is recorded in the Book of Daniel. He was the absolute monarch of the greatest empire of his day. It is hard for us to imagine the completeness of his power over the lives of his subjects. It has been said that power tends to corrupt, and that absolute power tends to corrupt absolutely. The graphic history of this Babylonian ruler illustrates this fact and the biblical truth that "pride goeth before destruction, and an haughty spirit before a fall" (Prov. 16:18). Nebuchadnezzar learned humility the hard way!

Nebuchadnezzar was a megalomaniac. A megalomaniac is a person who has delusions of power. However, Nebuchadnezzar's grandiose ideas about himself were not completely without foundation. He was a man of extraordinary energy, enterprise, and ability. He was an able military commander. He was an outstanding empire organizer and administrator. He built imposing public works on a grand scale. Under his leadership Babylon became one of the greatest cities of the ancient world. Its colossal, triple walls, impressive hanging gardens, and regal temples were among the "wonders of the world" at that time.

Our story of this unusual man must, however, bypass his achievements in military and political affairs. Instead, we will focus our attention on a moving personal drama in three acts.

ACT I: THE TROUBLED DREAMER

Nebuchadnezzar had a dream. This in itself is not so unusual, since he apparently dreamed quite frequently. But this dream was different. It was what might be called a nightmare. He awoke in a cold sweat, trembling with fear. Ordinarily a dreamer can recall at least the main theme of his dream. But not this dreamer! The content of the dream was completely repressed. Not even the symbols could be recalled. The anxiety-ridden king was deeply disturbed. What did the dream portend for the future?

So Nebuchadnezzar called for his retinue of prognosticators whose function was to interpret various omens, especially those presumably relating to future events. These magicians, soothsayers, sorcerers, enchanters, and wise men played an important role in Babylonian court life. The king depended on them to interpret the will of the gods concerning public policy.

Nebuchadnezzar lost no time in telling them of his traumatic dream. "But," he said, "the thing is gone from me." Their response was predictable: "O King, live forever. You tell us the dream, and we will give the interpretation."

However, the fiery and impatient despot would permit no excuse or delay. "If you do not tell me the dream and its interpretation you shall be hacked limb from limb, and your houses shall be made a dunghill!" To these threatening words, he then added his opinion that their excuses constituted only an effort to gain further time in the hope that some lucky event would serve their cause and save their necks. The magi still insisted that the king's request was highly irregular and unreasonable, a rare and unheard-of thing! "The solution to such a request," they argued, "lies only in the lap of the gods."

But Nebuchadnezzar was in no mood to listen to such reasoning. Beside himself with frustration and anger, he ordered the forthright execution of all the "wise men" of Babylon.

Daniel, God's loyal servant and one of Nebuchadnezzar's wise men, was not present during the foregoing stormy interview. When he heard of the king's impulsive decree, he requested a "stay of execution." This was granted. Daniel and his three faithful friends then prayed earnestly, and God made known the secret to Daniel in a night vision.

As usual, Daniel's first response was to offer praise and thanksgiving to God, saying: "Blessed be the name of God for ever and ever: for wisdom and might are his: and he changeth the times and the seasons: he removeth kings, and setteth up kings: he giveth wisdom unto the wise, and knowledge to them that know understanding" (Dan. 2: 20-21).

Daniel then came before the king, made known to him the contents of his forgotten dream, and interpreted its historical and prophetic meaning. Nebuchadnezzar's response to Daniel's interpretation was as sudden and impulsive as had been his hasty action toward the servile soothsayers. The despot fell on his face, worshipped Daniel, and commanded his servants to offer an oblation and sweet odors unto him. "Of a truth," said the megalomaniac, "it is, that your God is a God of gods, and a Lord of kings, and a revealer of secrets, seeing thou couldest reveal this secret."

But the despot's humility was superficial—as transient as the morning dew. It came from his lips but not from his will or heart. Events soon proved beyond doubt that Nebuchadnezzar had not yet learned that "pride goeth before destruction, and an haughty spirit before a fall" (Prov. 16:18).

ACT II: WORSHIP AS THE KING COMMANDS—OR ELSE!

The setting for Act II was the Plain of Dura, outside the majestic walls of Babylon. Nebuchadnezzar had made a great, golden image, 90 feet tall and nine feet in diameter. Whom did the image represent? The king himself? The god, Neb, after whom he had been named? Some other god of the Babylonian pantheon? We are not told. In any event, a solemn dedicatory ceremony was proclaimed. All major governmental officials were commanded to be present. Everything was prepared and carried out in Nebuchadnezzar's usual grandiose, flamboyant style. Was he already suffering from delusions of grandeur?

At the sound of the music from the royal orchestra with its cornets, flutes, harps, sackbuts, and psalters, all persons present were commanded to fall down and worship the golden image. A dire fate awaited all who failed or refused to obey the royal decree. They were "in that same hour to be cast into the midst of a burning fiery furnace."

For some reason, Daniel was not present on this dramatic occasion. But his brave, God-fearing friends— Shadrach, Meshach, and Abed-nego—were there. Their noncooperative behavior was immediately reported to the power-mad despot, Nebuchadnezzar. He was now suffering from an unusual attack of dizziness due to his perception of himself as absolute ruler. So he reacted with unrestrained fury. Their behavior, he asserted, was an insult to him and his gods. It was incredible, he declared, that the command of the master of the Babylonian Empire should be defied! And by three lowly, foreign captives at that! But he would be generous—give them one more chance to bow their knees. If they did not do so—into the furnace they would go. "And," shouted the overconfident king, "who is that god that shall deliver you out of my hands?"

All of us thrill at the display of quiet, moral courage by the three loyal Hebrew men who would not bow, and the account of their supernatural deliverance from the fiery furnace, heated to seven times its usual temperature.

Nebuchadnezzar's response to this remarkable deliverance was characteristically pious, yet superficial:

> Blessed be the god of Shadrach, Meshach, and Abednego, who hath sent his angel, and delivered his servants that trusted in him, and have changed the king's word, and yielded their bodies, that they might not serve nor worship any god, except their own God. Therefore I make a decree, That every people, nation, and language, which speak any thing amiss against the God of Shadrach, Meshach, and Abed-nego, shall be cut in pieces, and their houses shall be made a dunghill: because there is no other God that can deliver after this sort (Dan. 3:28-29).

But had Nebuchadnezzar really learned that "pride goeth before destruction, and an haughty spirit before a fall"? Act III will tell.

ACT III: THE HAUGHTY KING
WHO ATE GRASS LIKE AN OX

Twice Nebuchadnezzar had been led to recognize the existence and power of the true and living God. But his heart had never been truly humbled. Now he comes to a third and decisive experience, when he will personally acknowledge the sovereignty of Almighty God! It came as a lightning stroke of terrible personal calamity. However, a perceptive observer might have seen earlier evidences of an impending psychosis in his grandiose delusions and unpredictable, erratic behavior. One wonders, indeed, if the dissolute monarch had not been suffering for years from some sort of psychosis (expansive delusions of grandeur, and irrational, impulsive behavior).

The climactic events opened with a public proclamation:

> *Nebuchadnezzar the king, unto all people, nations, and languages, that dwell in all the earth; Peace be multiplied unto you. I thought it good to shew the signs and wonders that the high God hath wrought toward me. How great are his signs! and how mighty are his wonders! his kingdom is an everlasting kingdom, and his dominion is from generation to generation* (Dan. 4:1-3).

Nebuchadnezzar was at ease in his royal palace. Seemingly all was going well. But again he had a troublesome dream. This time he could remember the dream, but its meaning was obscure. Again the magicians and astrologers and soothsayers were called, but they could not interpret the dream. And again, it was Daniel, now given the Chaldean name Belteshazzar, who came to the king's assistance.

In the king's own words, this was his portentous dream:

> *I saw, and behold, a tree in the midst of the earth, and the height thereof was great. The tree grew, and was strong, and the height thereof reached unto heaven, and the sight thereof to the end of all the earth: the leaves thereof were fair, and the fruit thereof much, and in it was meat for all: the beasts of the field had shadow under it, and the fowls of the heaven dwelt in the boughs thereof, and all flesh was fed of it. . . .*
>
> *And, behold, a watcher and an holy one came down from heaven; he cried aloud, and said thus, Hew down the tree, and cut off his branches, shake off his leaves, and scatter his fruit: let the beasts get away from under it, and the fowls from his branches: Nevertheless leave the stump of his roots in the earth, even with a band of iron and brass, in the tender grass of the field; and let*

23

> it be wet with the dew of heaven, and let his portion be
> with the beasts in the grass of the earth: let his heart
> be changed from man's, and let a beast's heart be given
> unto him; and let seven times pass over him.
>
> This matter is by the decree of the watchers, and
> the demand by the word of the holy ones: to the intent
> that the living may know that the most High ruleth in
> the kingdom of men, and giveth it to whomsoever he
> will, and setteth up over it the basest of men (Dan. 4:
> 10-17).

Daniel quickly saw the meaning and design of the dream. He recognized at once its solemn significance for both Nebuchadnezzar and the empire. Only upon further urging by the king did he reveal the meaning, and then with delicacy, as well as courage: "My lord, the dream be to them that hate thee, and the interpretation thereof to thine enemies."

The great tree, said Daniel, represented the king himself, who had become so great and strong that his fame reached to heaven and his power to the ends of the earth. But the command of the "watcher" from heaven that the tree be cut down meant that he, Nebuchadnezzar, would be deposed and driven from men. He would make his home with the beasts of the field until he was willing to admit that the Almighty God was Ruler over all, including himself. The fact that the roots of the tree were to be left, signified that the kingdom would ultimately be restored after the king had come to this admission. Daniel urged the king to break off his sins and thus be spared the humiliation which was foretold.

But the haughty monarch did not heed the wise and fearless counsel of Daniel. A year later, Nebuchadnezzar was proudly walking in his palace congratulating himself: "Is not this great Babylon, that I have built for the house of the kingdom by the might of my power, and for the honour of my majesty?" (Dan. 4:30)

Then the predicted judgments of Almighty God fell like lightning:

> *While the word was in the king's mouth, there fell a voice from heaven, saying, O king Nebuchadnezzar, to thee it is spoken; The kingdom is departed from thee. And they shall drive thee from men, and thy dwelling shall be with the beasts of the field: they shall make thee to eat grass as oxen, and seven times shall pass over thee, until thou know that the most High ruleth in the kingdom of men, and giveth it to whomsoever he will* (Dan. 4:31-32).

So, in "the same hour was the thing fulfilled upon Nebuchadnezzar: and he was driven from men, and did eat grass as oxen, and his body was wet with the dew of heaven, till his hairs were grown like eagles' feathers and his nails like birds' claws" (v. 33).

The conclusion of the humiliation of Nebuchadnezzar is best described in his own words at the close of his seven-year mental illness:

> *At the end of the days I Nebuchadnezzar lifted up mine eyes unto heaven, and mine understanding returned unto me, and I blessed the most High, and I praised and honoured him that liveth for ever, whose dominion is an everlasting dominion, and his kingdom is from generation to generation: and all the inhabitants of the earth are reputed as nothing: and he doeth according to his will in the army of heaven, and among the inhabitants of the earth: and none can stay his hand, or say unto him, What doest thou? . . . Now I Nebuchadnezzar praise and extol and honour the King of heaven, all whose works are truth, and his ways judgment: and those that walk in pride he is able to abase* (vv. 34-37).

EPILOGUE

Nebuchadnezzar learned humility the hard way. Despite his success and the grandeur of his accomplishments and surroundings, he learned that he was not God. He was but a man who could not be certain of his own sanity! When he truly recognized the power and sovereignty of

25

Almighty God, his reason returned to him, and his return to power became possible.

Man was created by God as the culmination of a great creative plan. Then man was given dominion by his Creator over all that he surveyed. But as he looked up at his Creator, man's position was that of a steward or servant. The temptation of Satan was an appeal to man to defy his Creator, and deny his own servantship. Satan declared that man, by violating the specific commandment of God, would become a god, "knowing good from evil" (Gen. 3:5). But what the tempter did not tell man was that his lordship or dominion over nature was dependent on his continued, humble dependence upon his Creator.

So man yielded to the deceptive temptation of Satan. Man denied his stewardship and lost much of his lordship over nature. Sinful man lifts himself up in pride, as did Nebuchadnezzar, and pretends that he is a "god." It simply doesn't work. Nebuchadnezzar, and millions of other men who have learned humility the hard way, are examples of that fact. They have discovered that while the mills of the Sovereign God may grind slowly, they grind exceedingly fine.

What, then, is man's only hope? It is found in the One who was and is the majestic, eternal Son of the Living God. By Him, God created the vast universe, holds it in its integrity from moment to moment, and is directing it surely and relentlessly toward its divinely appointed destiny (Heb. 3:1-4; John 1:1-3). Out of His love for proud, sinful men, this One, who was Lord of all, humbled himself and became incarnate as the unique God-man. He further humbled himself and experienced all of our experiences, except sin, and finally suffered a shameful death on the Cross for you and me (Phil. 2:5-9). Why did He do all this? That He might provide the grace and power by which sinful man might be restored to something of his lost dominion and lordship.

26

The message of the Word of God to you and me is, "Let this mind be in you, which was also in Christ Jesus" (Phil. 2:5). Nebuchadnezzar's experience and testimony is that there is no desirable future in an attitude of pride which refuses to acknowledge the sovereignty and lordship of the God of heaven.

The Word of God declares with unmistakable clarity and certainty that "at the name of Jesus every knee . . . [shall] bow . . . and . . . every tongue . . . [shall] confess that Jesus Christ is Lord, to the glory of God the Father" (Phil. 2:10-11). The only question, then, is: Will our bowing be deliberate and voluntary, or will it be necessary for us, like Nebuchadnezzar, to learn humility the hard way?

3

RUTH:
Making the
Master Choices in Life

Just two books of the Bible are named after women: Ruth and Esther. One records the marriage of a Gentile girl to a Jew; and the other, the marriage of a Jewish girl to a Gentile monarch.

The Book of Ruth, only 85 verses in length, is considered one of the gems of world literature. It is a beautiful love story. The account gives a picture of simple rural life in an era of political chaos. It was during the period of the judges, when, as the Scriptures record, "every man did that which was right in his own eyes."

The names of Bible characters are often full of meaning and significance. The story recorded in the Book of Ruth is one of the most interesting illustrations of this fact.

Elimelech, whose name meant, "My God is King," and his wife, Naomi ("pleasantness"), left Bethlehem ("the house of bread") in time of famine and crossed the Jordan River to Moab, a heathen country. The Moabites, because of their ill treatment of the children of Israel on their journey from Egypt to Canaan, bore a special curse from God. No Moabite was to be permitted to enter the congregation of Israel to ten generations or "for ever." Was this move to Moab by Elimelech a result of lack of faith in God's providential care? Did he forget that God was King? In any event, life soon lost its pleasantness, not only for Naomi, but for the entire family.

Elimelech and Naomi had two sons. Neither of the boys seemingly had very good health, for one was named Mahlon ("sick") and the other, Chilion ("pining" or "puny"). Some time after the family arrived in Moab, Elimelech died. The two boys then married young women (possibly sisters) of Moab, Ruth ("friendship") and Orpah ("youthful freshness"). In about 10 years both Mahlon and Chilion died. Naomi was now bereft of both husband and sons, and was probably poverty-stricken as well. Discouraged and disillusioned, her heart was filled with remorse and regret and self-pity.

Hearing that there was again plenty to eat in Bethlehem, "the house of bread and peace," Naomi decided to return to her native land. Her two daughters-in-law accompanied her on the road toward Judea. She repeatedly urged them to return to their own land and their mothers' homes, in order that they might remarry and start life anew. They wept aloud and declared, "No, we will go back with you to your people." But Naomi insisted on their return, and pointed out the futility of outcasts like themselves remaining in Israel. In support of her argument she asserted that even God was against her. "The hand of God is gone out against me," she said bitterly.

At length, Orpah kissed Naomi good-bye and turned back to her own people and their heathen gods. But Ruth clung to her beloved mother-in-law. Naomi called her attention to Orpah's decision to return. Then Ruth, a simple, unlettered, country girl, made one of the greatest state-

29

ments of all time. It was but a single, balanced, beautiful sentence, which is really a poem. It was actually the only significant recorded statement of this attractive young woman. On it her fame largely rests. Note it carefully:

> And Ruth said, Entreat me not to leave thee, or to return from following after thee: for whither thou goest, I will go; and where thou lodgest, I will lodge: thy people shall be my people, and thy God my God: where thou diest, will I die, and there will I be buried: the Lord do so to me, and more also, if aught but death part thee and me (Ruth 1:16-17).

Ruth's great statement is one of the most significant and moving decisions ever recorded at the crossroads of a person's life. And it is what people say and do at the crossroads which reveals what they are, and determines what they will become. Such discriminating decisiveness marks Ruth as an exceptionally mature person—at least by this important criterion.

Ruth's decision was wholehearted, personal, and courageous. It was voluntary—made in the face of two or more contrary pleas from her esteemed older companion. An irrevocable, final, life-changing, master choice, her decision involved the greatest of life's issues: personal relationships, racial and national ties and loyalties, and fidelity to the true and living God of Israel. It was doubtless made in the light of some knowledge concerning the issues involved, but was also made in faith, with no certain knowledge of what the future held as a result of the drastic step she was taking.

William James, the outstanding philosopher, psychologist, and educator of the last generation, has said that every decision partakes of three of six characteristics. It is living or dead, trivial or momentous, and forced or avoidable. Ruth's decision to identify herself with God and His people was a living, momentous, and forced decision. It was *living*, in that she realized to some degree what the

30

issues were and how they would inescapably influence her personally. The decision was *momentous* in that it involved life's greatest values, and all other subsequent decisions of her life would be influenced by it. It was a *forced* decision because no neutral position was possible; it was either go forward with Naomi and her God or turn back to the outcast land of Moab with its heathen darkness.

The story does not reveal all the factors which led Ruth to make this wise, discriminating, momentous choice. However, there is a strong suggestion that the godly counsel and example of her mother-in-law played a major role. The relationship between the older and the younger woman was exceptionally close and marked by mutual regard and deep affection. Later on in the story the women of Bethlehem spoke appreciatively to Naomi about Ruth: "Your daughter-in-law who loves you, who is more to you than seven sons." Little wonder, then, that Ruth declared, "Thy God shall be my God." By example and counsel Naomi had won Ruth to faith in the true and living God.

Ruth's choice was made in total ignorance of the happy and blessed consequences which were to follow in her life, and in the lives of countless other people. The Book of Ruth records her subsequent romance and marriage to Boaz, one of the leading citizens of Bethlehem, who became a type of the Lord Jesus Christ as the Kinsman-Redeemer. To this union was born a son, who became the grandfather of Israel's greatest king, David. And through this relationship, Ruth became one of the human ancestors of our Lord, and one of the four Gentile women named in the genealogy of Christ as given by St. Matthew. What a momentous choice—in the light of its glorious and enduring consequences!

Not only is intelligent decisiveness an evidence of a healthy personality, but a great, master motive, such as that of Ruth, is also a key to successful living. A master

31

motive adds an element of unity to the personality, and gives a sense of purpose or directedness to the whole of a person's life.

Such a master purpose helps in many ways. Robert was an above-average college student, but was certainly no intellectual genius. He had a good mind, but was not brilliant. But he had one great asset: a consuming desire to become a great neurosurgeon. This driving motive influenced his total life as a student and as a person.

He studied hard and efficiently in every course. He used his imagination to borrow motivation from his challenging life goal. Even in the required courses which seemed so unrelated to being a competent doctor, he got his assignments in on time, did extra reading, and took the unwelcome examinations on schedule. He even developed quite an interest in several courses which most students thought of as "dull."

Robert often studied while other so-called students loafed, played, or slept. He was an academic success, graduating with high honors. He was among the top two or three in his class in medical school. Today he is busy serving his Lord, needy people, and his country with devotion and distinction.

And why? Not because he had exceptional talent. Nor was he a "born student," as some envious fellows seemed to think. No, his secret was that he had a compelling, overriding, master motive. In contrast to some of his more competent fellow students who were relative failures, Robert was never content with immediate results—such as they were. He paid the price of daily self-discipline, not because it came naturally or was easy. Rather, he paid the price of this daily grind because he knew—as do all others who stop to think—that this was the *only way* to attain his long-term goal of being a competent neurosurgeon.

Some years ago, Albert E. N. Gray worked with hundreds of life insurance salesmen. He believed that the same principle which Robert followed is the fundamental difference between those who succeed or fail as salesmen. Here is the way Gray puts it, "As long as you live don't ever forget that while you may succeed beyond your fondest hopes and your greatest expectations, you will never succeed beyond the purpose to which you are willing to surrender. Furthermore, your surrender will not be complete until you have formed the habit of doing the things that failures don't like to do." And my experience with thousands of college students over almost four decades of teaching leads me to the same conclusion.

But the same principle is equally applicable to the Christian life. A total personal commitment of love and loyalty to the Lord Jesus Christ and His way is what we need for victorious and effective Christian living. And Ruth's great decision, though she lived before the Christian era, points the way for you and me.

In the early days of World War II an English boy, Jack Riley, was being sent to Canada for safety. In the cold, early morning hours of a bleak November day the ship on which he was traveling was torpedoed in the North Atlantic. Somehow, Jack got hold of a bit of wreckage and at length was picked up by some survivors in a lifeboat. One would have thought that his first remarks would have been a plea for his mother, or an expression of regret for ever having left England. Not so with Jack Riley. His first words were, "Which way is America?"

He had set out with a purpose to arrive in America, and no mere shipwreck was to turn him aside.

And so it was with Ruth. Her master choice suggests that she had caught that vision splendid: "Thy God shall be my God." And nothing was to turn her aside from an identification with God, His purposes, and His people. And the blessed and deathless consequences of her wise and decisive choice suggest comparable master choices for you and me.

4

BALAAM:
Challenging the Occult

For thousands of years, people have been intrigued by what may be called the "spiritual underworld." This is the realm of the occult. A lively discussion usually occurs when the subject of ghosts, hexing, witching, or communication with the dead is mentioned.

The realm of the occult includes also such phenomena as astrology, demon possession, and the worship of Satan. Modern devotees of these "black arts" include witch doctors, fortune-tellers, and mediums. In the Old Testament such terms as enchanters, diviners, wizards, sorcerers, necromancers, and soothsayers are used.

The Word of God contains stern warnings and prohibitions against dealing with the demonic forces of the occult. As the children of Israel were about to settle in the land of Canaan, this warning was given to them by the Lord:

> When thou art come into the land which the Lord thy God giveth thee, thou shalt not learn to do after the abominations of those nations. There shall not be found among you any one that maketh his son or daughter to pass through the fire, or that useth divination, or an observer of times, or an enchanter, or a witch, or a charmer, or a consulter with familiar spirits, or a wizard, or a necromancer. For all that do these things are an abomination unto the Lord: and because of these abominations the Lord thy God doth drive them out from before thee. Thou shalt be perfect with the Lord thy God. For these nations, which thou shalt possess, hearkened unto observers of times, and unto diviners: but as for thee, the Lord thy God hath not suffered thee so to do (Deut. 18:9-14).

Saul, Israel's first king, presumably carried out a campaign to rid the nation of mediums possessing "familiar spirits." And yet in a time of personal and national crisis, Saul sought out the witch of En-dor. He hoped, through her, to obtain guidance from the deceased prophet, Samuel.

Today there is widespread interest in the occult. Daily papers carry horoscopes and astrological charts to which thousands of persons turn for guidance.

People who are in trouble or who are bereaved turn to mediums for some word of hope or encouragement from those who have died. There is a lady in Los Angeles who claims to be the city's official "witch"; and the cult of Satanic worship, with its dark and mysterious rites, flourishes in our society. The late Bishop Pike claimed that he was able to communicate with the spirit of his deceased son.

But the black arts of the occult have a long and devious history. The dark and mysterious character Balaam, who is the subject of this study, lived a long time ago. He was a *diviner* or *soothsayer* (Josh. 13:22; Num. 23:23). He was *never* called a prophet of God. And yet the Bible declares that on several occasions "God came to him," or that he

35

spoke by divine inspiration. In fact his prophecies, including a remarkable one concerning the coming of Christ, are among the most beautiful and inspiring in the entire Bible. It is even possible, though not at all certain, that Balaam may have been the author of what is generally conceded to be the finest definition of true religion in the Old Testament: "He hath shewed thee, O man, what is good; and what doth the Lord require of thee, but to do justly, and to love mercy, and to walk humbly with thy God?" (Mic. 6:8) Clovis G. Chappell refers to Balaam as the "Angelic Devil," an extremely apt description of this man of complex character and mixed motives. Balaam fits the characterization of the Apostle James as a "double-minded man . . . unstable in all his ways." A clever genius, he possessed poetic gifts of a very high order.

Balaam has also been called the "Rogue of Revelation." A study of his personality and behavior is of interest for several reasons: the fact that he was a soothsayer, his complex motive life, and his efforts to twist his conscience to attain his desires for prestige and financial reward. Yet he was a rascal at heart, with an overweening desire for material gain. There is a striking similarity between Balaam and Judas Iscariot, who sold our Lord for 30 pieces of silver. Concerning each, it was said that he went to his own place.

The Word of God gives a surprising amount of space to the story of Balaam. Almost all of chapters 22 to 24 in the Book of Numbers are devoted to him and his remarkable prophecies. He is mentioned in several other books of the Old Testament as well as by Jude, Peter, and John in the New Testament.

In their journey from Egypt to Canaan, the children of Israel had moved north along the east side of the Dead Sea. The Moabites and Midianites, who lived in this general area, had already heard of the miraculous way in which

God had delivered His people from their enemies. The result was that the people of Moab and their king, Balak, were "sore afraid" (22:3). Balak therefore sent messengers to Balaam in Pethor (in Mesopotamia) to seek his help. His plea was:

> Behold, there is a people come out from Egypt: behold, they cover the face of the earth, and they abide over against me: come now therefore, I pray thee, curse me this people; for they are too mighty for me: peradventure I shall prevail, that we may smite them, and that I may drive them out of the land: for I wot [know] that he whom thou blessest is blessed, and he whom thou cursest is cursed (22:5-6).

So the elders of Midian and Moab came to Balaam with "the rewards of divination in their hands" (22:7). They delivered the request of King Balak. Balaam replied: "Lodge here this night, and I will bring you word again, as the Lord shall speak unto me" (22:8).

The word of the Lord to Balaam was clear and decisive, "Thou shalt not go with them; thou shalt not curse the people: for they are blessed" (22:12). This clear word Balaam passed on to the ambassadors of Balak, "Get you into your land: for the Lord refuseth to give me leave to go with you" (22:13). And so the envoys returned to Moab.

But King Balak was a persistent man. He sent a still more impressive delegation to Balaam. Balak's urgent message through them was, "Let nothing, I pray thee, hinder thee from coming unto me: for I will promote thee unto very great honour, and I will do whatsoever thou sayest unto me: come therefore, I pray thee, curse me this people" (22:16).

Balaam's reply reveals both his character weakness and moral vulnerability. He exaggerates in a flamboyant way. He overcompensates, revealing his overpowering desire for money. "If Balak would give me his house full of silver and gold, I cannot go beyond the word of the Lord my God, to do less or more" (22:18). On the surface, this sounds very pious! But look out! He is talking too loud!

The word of the Lord had already been unequivocal, simple, and clear: *"Do not go."* But Balaam's mixed motives caused him to dally. So his response was, "Tarry ye . . . here this night, that I may know what the Lord will say unto me more" (22:19). By morning he was "convinced" that God had changed His mind. So the revised instructions apparently came, "If the men come to call thee, rise up, and go with them; but yet the word which I shall say unto thee, that shalt thou do" (22:20).

In the morning there is no suggestion that Balaam waited for anyone to call him. He immediately rose up and went. And God's anger was kindled against him because he went, and the angel of the Lord stood in his way as an adversary. When Balaam saw the angel of the Lord, he bowed his head and fell flat on his face. The angel's message to him was, "Thy way is perverse before me." Balaam's response was, "I have sinned . . . if it displease thee, I will get me back again" (22:32-34).

What does all this mean? Is it not evidence that Balaam was playing fast and loose with his conscience? He knew what was right. But his driving ambition and desire for wealth blinded him to the clear command of Almighty God.

So Balaam came to Balak. Three times, on three different high places overlooking the encampment of Israel, Balak erected altars and offered sacrifices for Balaam, vainly hoping that he would curse God's people. But on each occasion the Lord commanded Balaam to bless rather than curse His people.

Standing on the first mountain, Balaam declared:

> *How shall I curse, whom God hath not cursed? or how shall I defy, whom the Lord hath not defied? For from the top of the rocks I see him, and from the hills I behold him: lo, the people shall dwell alone, and shall not be reckoned among the nations. Who can count the*

> *dust of Jacob, and the number of the fourth part of Israel?*
> *Let me die the death of the righteous, and let my last*
> *end be like his!* (23:8-10)

What a remarkable prophecy and worthy wish for an angel/devil to utter!

Balak apparently anticipated that a different perspective might alter the blessing into cursing! It was a futile hope! So from a second mountain Balaam declared:

> *God is not a man, that he should lie; neither the son*
> *of man, that he should repent: hath he said, and shall*
> *he not do it? or hath he spoken, and shall he not make it*
> *good? Behold, I have received commandment to bless:*
> *and he hath blessed; and I cannot reverse it. He hath not*
> *beheld iniquity in Jacob, neither hath he seen perverse-*
> *ness in Israel: the Lord his God is with him, and the shout*
> *of a king is among them. God brought them out of Egypt;*
> *he hath as it were the strength of an unicorn. Surely there*
> *is no enchantment against Jacob, neither is there any*
> *divination against Israel: according to this time it shall*
> *be said of Jacob and of Israel, What hath God wrought!*
> (23:19-23)

Balak was disgusted but he determined to try once more. So he took Soothsayer Balaam to a third vantage point overlooking the hosts of Israel. Again the result was the same: blessing instead of cursing.

> *How goodly are thy tents, O Jacob, and thy taber-*
> *nacles, O Israel! As the valleys are they spread forth, as*
> *gardens by the river's side, as the trees of the lign aloes*
> *which the Lord hath planted, and as cedar trees beside the*
> *waters* (24:5-6).

Balak by now had had enough. He slapped his fist into his hand and ordered the obstinate, uncooperative prophet to return home.

But Balaam didn't leave until he had given one more remarkable prophecy. It concerned the coming of our Lord Jesus Christ, and the star which should herald His birth. What an incredible fact that such a sublime prophecy should have come by the mouth of a heathen soothsayer!

39

> *I shall see him, but not now: I shall behold him, but not nigh: there shall come a Star out of Jacob, and a Sceptre shall rise out of Israel, and shall smite the corners of Moab, and destroy all the children of Sheth. And Edom shall be a possession, Seir also shall be a possession for his enemies; and Israel shall do valiantly. Out of Jacob shall come he that shall have dominion, and shall destroy him that remaineth of the city* (24:17-19).

So Balaam returned home. Each time he was urged to curse God's people, he uttered a blessing instead! But, unfortunately and tragically, this wasn't the end of the story. Balaam, the soothsayer, returned home still lusting in his heart for the honors and riches which Balak had offered to him.

In Numbers, chapter 25, we find a sad story in which the people of Israel, the very people whom Balak wanted to curse and destroy, were enticed into participating in the lewd, idolatrous, sensuous feasts of the Moabites. The result was awful physical, moral, and spiritual corruption. How did this tragic thing happen to God's people? In Num. 31:16, we read, "Behold, these [women of Moab] caused the children of Israel, through the counsel of Balaam, to commit trespass against the Lord in the matter of Peor." As a result of this horrible sexual debauchery, a plague (possibly of VD) was visited upon Israel and 24,000 men died.

Balaam, who refused to curse Israel in *word*, became, through his counsel of alliance with the sensual pagan people of Moab, the worst kind of curse to God's people. Little wonder that Balaam is consistently cited in the New Testament as a man who compromised truth, virtue, and righteousness for material gain!

The strange complexity of Balaam's motives and the resulting instability in his life are reflected even in his death. At one time he had prayed, with at least a curious show of sincerity, "Let me die the death of the righteous, and let my end be like his!" But this high aspiration was a far cry from his actual end.

To avenge the physical, moral, and spiritual seduction of Israel, which came through Balaam's counsel, God commanded the Israelites to take up arms against the Moabites and Midianites. In this campaign, five princes were slain. And among them was Balaam, the soothsayer, the son of Beor.

What shall we think of this strange man, Balaam? It is doubtful whether the Word of God presents a more complex character. He is full of mystery. What was his background? How did he ever come to know of and communicate with the true and living God? Several times it is recorded that "God came to him," that "God put words in his mouth," or that the "Spirit of God came upon him." As we have seen, he usually *spoke* God's message. Yet one wonders whether or not he was secretly hoping that God would allow him to curse Israel and gain the honors and riches which he madly coveted.

In the end he brought a curse upon Israel by his counsel of alliance with the impure, idolatrous Midianites. To this extent he gained his primary objective. But he gained neither riches nor honors. And he failed to die the death of the righteous!

The Apostle Peter, speaking of false prophets and teachers, compares them to Balaam: "Which have forsaken the right way, and are gone astray, following the way of Balaam the son of Bosor, who loved the wages of unrighteousness; but was rebuked for his iniquity: the dumb ass speaking with man's voice forbad the madness of the prophet" (II Pet. 2:15-16).

Jude, one of our Lord's brethren, also referring to apostate leaders, warned, "Woe unto them! for they have gone in the way of Cain, and ran greedily after the error of Balaam for reward" (Jude 11).

The Apostle John, recording the message of the risen,

glorified Christ to the church in Pergamos, wrote, "I have a few things against thee, because thou hast there them that hold the doctrine of Balaam, who taught Balac to cast a stumblingblock before the children of Israel, to eat things sacrificed unto idols, and to commit fornication" (Rev. 2:14).

These three New Testament writers refer, respectively, to the *way* of Balaam, the *error* of Balaam, and the *doctrine* of Balaam. The *doctrine of Balaam* is clear; it is the effort to fuse the truth and purity of God with idolatry and uncleanness. It is to violate the principle of Christian separation from a sensual, pagan, evil world-order.

The *error of Balaam* seems to have been his persistent, unexpressed opinion that somehow, through continued effort, he could gain God's permission to curse the people of God. But he didn't really know God! God could be severe in His judgments, but He wasn't going to let a heathen soothsayer sit in judgment on His people and curse them. Never!

The *way of Balaam* appears to be related to his "money madness." Peter declares that Balaam "loved the wages of unrighteousness." His persistent motivation was to compromise the truth for personal prestige and financial gain. His "way" was his life-style.

But underlying Balaam's "error" and "doctrine" and "way" was a condition of mixed motivation. He was trying to do the impossible: serve both God and mammon! He needed an effective integration of his inner motivational life around some supreme, master motive.

Whatever and whoever enables a person to harmonize his powers, focus his energies, and channel his efforts toward high and worthy goals is a great benefactor. Our Lord Jesus Christ proposes to do this for you and me—on life's highest level. By His grace and power working in our lives, and by the acceptance of His will as our master motive, a basic integration is achieved which must then be developed

42

and enhanced by the process of growth in grace toward Christian maturity.

We need not, like Balaam, go through life with a basic inner conflict concerning our ultimate, spiritual loyalty. General William Booth, founder of the Salvation Army, declared that the secret of his unusually happy and useful life was that "Jesus Christ has had all there was of me."

The baton of the Master will hush the jangling discords of our lives. Life can become the music of God. After the vision had passed on the Mount of Transfiguration, the disciples "saw no man, save Jesus only." He filled their horizon. He can fill ours. Like the Apostle Paul, we shall then discover that all things cohere in Him.

5

JABEZ:
Overcoming the Shadows of the Past

Hidden away within the longest genealogical table of the Old Testament is one of the short but meaningful biographies for which the Bible is justly famous. Here is the entire life-story as recorded in I Chron. 4:9-10:

> *And Jabez was more honourable than his brethren: and his mother called his name Jabez, saying, Because I bare him with sorrow. And Jabez called on the God of Israel, saying, Oh that thou wouldest bless me indeed, and enlarge my coast, and that thine hand might be with me, and that thou wouldest keep me from evil, that it may not grieve me! And God granted him that which he requested.*

One of the curious things about this short story is that, while it is given in the midst of a genealogical table, the ancestry of Jabez is not mentioned. Consequently there is some mystery about him. However, we do know that a city of the scribes was named after him. Some historians believe that he was an eminent doctor of the law. Others think that he was a leader in the conquest of Canaan.

Evidence strongly indicates that Jabez was a Kenite, a descendant of the Rechabites. The latter consisted of a group of highly disciplined, virtuous people. The group was founded by Jonadab, the son of Rechab. Their founder commanded them to dwell in tents, and abstain from all intoxicants. For generations, the group maintained its simplicity of life and strength of moral character.

On one occasion God used the Rechabites to communicate a message of reproof to Israel. At the command of God the prophet Jeremiah tested the Rechabites by offering them strong drink. Their refusal to imbibe proved that they were still holding firmly to their original ideals, convictions, and vows. Their steadfast loyalty was to the commands of their founder, Jonadab. Jeremiah held up their behavior as an object lesson to Israel, who had neglected and disregarded God's laws. The divine promise was that the Rechabites would be amply rewarded for their steadfast loyalty to high values. They would not "want a man to stand before" the Lord of hosts forever. Thus, while we do not know the exact ancestry of Jabez, we are quite sure that he was one of these Rechabites—a clean-living, God-fearing, high-thinking, self-disciplined man.

The Rechabites represent the kind of ancestry of which any man might be justifiably proud. The English poet and hymn writer, William Cowper, expresses this thought in these lines:

> My boast is not, that I deduce my birth
> From loins enthroned, or rulers of the earth;
> But higher far my proud pretensions rise—
> The son of parents passed into the skies.

The short, short biography of Jabez suggests that he

began life with a handicap. His name means "pain" or "sorrow." We are told that his mother so named him because she "bare him with sorrow." Birth is often a painful and severe crisis. We usually think of it as a crisis for the mother. So it is! But it is equally, or even more, hazardous to the infant. One careful study showed the presence of blood in the spinal fluid of 20 percent of a large sample of newborn babies. This points to the possible injury of a considerable number of them.

Of course, the common view that birth is a crisis in the life of a mother is well grounded in fact. Yet, in spite of the travail of the birth experience, the sorrow is usually quickly forgotten in the joy that a child has been born into the world. But not in the case of the mother of Jabez! For some reason this boy was named after the sorrowful, painful birth-experience of his mother!

We are not told why this was done. The period of her labor may have been long and exhausting. Perhaps the mother, being somewhat morbid, wanted to "enjoy" herself by persistently reminding herself of her sorrow. Possibly she wanted to impress Jabez with the serious fact of his "existential" situation—that his days would be short, and full of trouble and sorrow. It may be that she wanted to remind him of his lasting indebtedness to her for his very existence.

Whatever the reason for naming Jabez after the unhappy circumstances surrounding his painful birth, his name, like some of ours, was a handicap to him. It reminded him of his "shadow." This is intimated in his extraordinary prayer in which he asks God to deliver him from evil "that it may not grieve [or pain] me!" He apparently did not want to become a lived-out illustration of his name.

Despite his "shadow," Jabez, with divine help, was able to become an overcomer. Others were honorable, but he was "more honourable." He lived nobly and usefully.

His example is an encouragement to all who are handicapped by some shadow in their past.

And that probably includes all of us. Yes, we do have shadows for which we need God's healing word. Our shadows are many and varied: some tragic sin or mistake, forgiven and "forgotten" by God, but not by us; an emotional wound inflicted in childhood; a persistent, morbid, irrational fear whose original cause has long since been forgotten; a romance which collapsed because of the influence of evil or weak persons, or by reason of circumstances over which we had no control; an untimely and seemingly tragic death of a loved one; a weak, punishing conscience growing out of inadequate training in childhood. What resources does the Christian faith offer for creatively and courageously meeting the challenge of these and other similar "shadows"?

For the shadow of guilt cast by our sins, there is the glorious deliverance of a free and complete pardon. "All [of us] have sinned, and come short of the glory of God." But there was One, even the Lord Jesus Christ, who suffered on the cross of Calvary that we might be completely forgiven. "If we confess our sins, he is faithful and just to forgive us our sins" (I John 1:9). "Therefore being justified by faith, we have peace with God through our Lord Jesus Christ" (Rom. 5:1). Yes, our sins may be forgiven, the guilt remitted, and the penalty canceled! The glorious promise of God is: "Though your sins be as scarlet, they shall be as white as snow; though they be red like crimson, they shall be as wool" (Isa. 1:18). The Psalmist exultantly declares, "For as the heaven is high above the earth, so great is his mercy toward them that fear him. As far as the east is from the west, so far hath he removed our transgressions from us" (Ps. 103:11-12).

Then there are the shadows cast by our weakness. We may hurt ourselves or others, not because we intend to, but because we fail under pressure. The demands of life are

47

too much for us. We disappoint ourselves, and others. We develop unwholesome, negative attitudes toward ourselves.

For the shadows cast by weakness there is the adequacy of the fullness of the Holy Spirit. Those who walk daily in the Spirit and under His guidance find the key to victorious Christian living. They are saved by the resurrected life of Christ (Rom. 5:10), and become more than conquerors by the power of the indwelling Spirit of Christ.

They have more adequate self-images, for they can now accept themselves because they are "accepted in the beloved" (Eph. 1:6; Rom. 12:3). They need not live with a sense of self-blame or self-disparagement because of the failures and regrets of the past. Yes, in the fullness of the Spirit, and a daily walk in the Spirit, there is an answer to the shadows cast by weakness and past failure.

Such a Spirit-filled, Spirit-led person can now plan creatively for the future and make the very most of present opportunities. The Apostle Paul, who had dark shadows in his past, had found this secret of dealing with "shadows": "Forgetting what is behind me, and reaching out for that which lies ahead, I press towards the goal to win the prize which is God's call to the life above, in Christ Jesus" (Phil. 3:13-14, NEB). The wise man of old declared that "the path of the just is as the shining light, that shineth more and more unto the perfect day" (Prov. 4:18).

The following bit of verse, while expressing certain questionable pantheistic concepts, puts emphasis on the thought of making the most of the present moment and its opportunities for growth and service. It was written by the Indian poet Kalidasa:

SALUTATION TO THE DAWN
Look to this Day,
For it is life, the very breath of life.
In its brief course lie all the
Realities of your Existence:

The Bliss of Growth,
The Glory of Action,
The Splendour of Beauty;
For yesterday is only a dream
And tomorrow is only a vision,
But today, well lived,
Makes every tomorrow a vision of hope,
And every yesterday a dream of happiness.
Look well, therefore, to this day.

As we face the shadows of our past, let us never under-estimate what God is able to do with the most sordid and tragic events of life. He can take the "lead" of life and trans-mute it into "gold." Is not this exactly what He did when His only begotten Son was arraigned unjustly, tried unfair-ly, and murdered on a cross? The world's supreme tragedy became man's hope for salvation! God can do something comparable with the seemingly tragic events in your life and mine if we will but give Him a chance. With Him, problems always equal opportunities!

Lastly, like Jabez, we should seek for and find the heal-ing which comes through fervent, believing prayer. The prayer of Jabez is one of the most beautiful and meaningful recorded in the Scriptures. Prayer was doubtless a major key to his triumphant and "more honorable" living. Such prayer can do the same for you and me.

Jabez prayed to the true and living God, who hears and answers prayer. He might have turned to the popular gods of the Canaanites: Baal, Ashtoreth, Moloch. But Jabez had the wisdom to seek the favor and help of the true and living God of Israel, the God who makes and keeps covenants, and who hears and answers prayer.

Jabez prayed in the spirit of sincere earnestness. His prayer came "from his heart." The language is that of ser-ious petition: "Oh that thou wouldest bless me indeed!" Here is the spirit of ardent devotion and affectionate desire.

49

The words imply a pledge of fidelity, of faithful and sincere response.

The order of the requests and the content of the prayer of Jabez are meaningful, and instructive. First is a petition for God's overflowing blessing on his own heart and life. He who is thus blessed is blessed indeed. The heart of true religion is the religion of the heart. Jabez then prayed that the Lord God would "enlarge my coast." This is a request that his influence for good might be extended. Those whose hearts are blessed of God to overflowing may well request that the scope of their influence be enlarged. Then Jabez prayed that the hand of God be with him. God's "hand" symbolizes His interest, support, guidance, restraint, leadership, and protection. The Scriptures declare that God's children are graven on His hands. We, like Jabez, need so very much that the hand of God be with us. Finally, Jabez prayed that God would keep him from evil, that it might not grieve him. We are reminded of the prayer of a greater than Jabez who taught us to pray, ". . . and deliver us from evil." Moral evil is the supreme hazard from which we need deliverance. Jabez was right; it is evil that really grieves or pains. Yes, our prayer should include an earnest request to be delivered from all that is truly evil.

When Jabez prayed, earnestly, unselfishly, and in faith, God answered. The account is majestic in its simplicity: "And God granted him that which he requested." Despite his shadow, Jabez lived more honorably than his contemporaries. He overcame the shadow in his past, and God answered his unselfish prayer. And He will do the same for each and all who follow the example of the man whose very name reminded him of his shadow.

6

JOASH:
The Danger of Falling Away

The life of Joash, famous boy-king of Judah, presents us with a unique problem in the development of moral character. How can we explain the fact that a person may consistently follow a certain course of moral conduct for years, and then suddenly and completely do an about-face? For many years Joash gave many evidences of being a noble, honorable, God-fearing ruler. Then he suddenly became an idolater and committed a dastardly crime—one that was almost unthinkable according to minimal standards of compassion and decency. Why? How did it happen? His story proves that a crucial defect can occur in the development of the moral character of an apparently "good" man.

Jehoram, the grandfather of Joash, was a ruthless and

51

evil king. He murdered all of his brothers, and married Athaliah, a woman known for her incredibly evil ways. Her evil deeds equalled, and possibly surpassed, those of her infamous and better known mother, Jezebel.

Jehoram reigned for eight years, until the judgment of God in the form of an intestinal disease caught up with him. At the end of an illness of two years, "his bowels came out because of the disease, and he died in great agony" (II Chron. 21:19, RSV). The Word of God declares that Jehoram "departed with no one's regret." What an epitaph!

Jehoram was succeeded on the throne by his son Ahaziah, who subsequently became the father of Joash. Ahaziah's reign, like that of his father, Jehoram, was marked by its unusually wicked character. Fortunately it lasted only one year. Ahaziah was slain by the hard-driving Jehu, who was in the process of executing the judgment of God upon the household of Ahab and Jezebel, wicked rulers of Israel, the Northern Kingdom.

When Athaliah, Ahaziah's mother and the diabolical wife of the deceased Jehoram, heard of her son's unexpected death at the hands of Jehu, she felt that her big chance had come. So she proceeded to murder all of the royal family that she could get her blood-stained hands on. But this she-devil failed to take into account the resourcefulness and courage of her daughter Jehoshabeath. Jehoshabeath was the wife of a devout priest, Jehoiada, who supported his wife in her daring venture.

They stole the infant son of the dead king from among his children who were about to be liquidated *en masse* by their bloodthirsty grandmother. The stolen infant, Joash, and his nurse were hidden, of all places, in the Temple of God! Presumably they knew that the Temple would be about the last place in the world where Athaliah would likely go.

For the next six years the monstrous Athaliah reigned

unchallenged in Judah. Then Jehoiada, the priest, made his big move. He carefully and secretly organized the Levites, priests, and other national leaders, and a *coup d'etat* was thoroughly planned. At the appointed time Joash, now seven years of age, was brought into the Temple court, crowned with appropriate ceremonies, and the attendants shouted, "Long live the king." Queen Athaliah was taken completely by surprise and in appropriately dramatic style shouted, "Treason, Treason." Jehoiada was well prepared for all eventualities, including the summary execution of Athaliah outside the Temple precincts at the entrance of the horse gate of the king's house.

Jehoiada then made a covenant between himself, the people of Judah, and the boy king that "they should be the Lord's people." The worship of the Lord's house was purified, idolatry was at least partially put down, and the land prospered under the new leadership.

Joash began to reign when he was seven years of age, and reigned for 40 years in Jerusalem. "And Joash did what was right in the eyes of the Lord all the days of Jehoiada the priest" (II Chron. 24:2).

At the appropriate time, Jehoiada obtained two wives for the young king, and the latter had sons and daughters.

Joash took a vital interest in the restoration of the Temple of the Lord, and the worship of God. In fact, he was more concerned with the progress of this work than his older priestly adviser, Jehoiada. The king arranged for more adequate financial support for the Temple worship, and the work of restoration and repair went forward at his urging.

Now comes the turning point in the strange career of Joash. Jehoiada died at the ripe age of 130 and was given a state burial in the City of David among the kings because of his great contribution to the people of Israel. It was the end of an era and marked a complete change in Joash:

> Now after the death of Jehoiada the princes of Judah
> came and did obeisance to the king; then the king

> hearkened to them. And they forsook the house of the Lord, the God of their fathers, and served the Asherim and the idols. And wrath came upon Judah and Jerusalem for this their guilt. Yet he sent prophets among them . . . but they would not give heed. Then the Spirit of God took possession of Zechariah the son of Jehoiada the priest; and he stood above the people, and said to them, "Thus says God, 'Why do you transgress the commandments of the Lord, so that you cannot prosper? Because you have forsaken the Lord, he has forsaken you.'" But they conspired against him, and by command of the king they stoned him with stones in the court of the house of the Lord. Thus Joash the king did not remember the kindness which Jehoiada, Zechariah's father, had shown him, but killed his son. And when he was dying, he said, "May the Lord see and avenge!" (II Chron. 24:17-22, RSV)

The Lord did see, and vengeance was not long in coming:

> At the end of the year the army of the Syrians came up against Joash. They came to Judah and to Jerusalem, and destroyed all the princes of the people from among the people, and sent all their spoil to the king of Damascus. Though the army of the Syrians had come with few men, the Lord delivered into their hand a very great army, because they had forsaken the Lord, the God of their fathers. Thus they executed judgment on Joash. When they had departed from him, leaving him severely wounded, his servants conspired against him because of the blood of the son of Jehoiada the priest, and slew him on his bed. So he died; and they buried him in the city of David, but they did not bury him in the tombs of the kings (II Chron. 24:23-25, RSV).

Joash owed his very life to Jehoshabeath and Jehoiada. They rescued him as an infant from the murderous terror of Athaliah; reared him as a child, hazarding their very lives in doing so. Then, with great daring and skill, they made possible his elevation to the throne of Judah. Yet he ruthlessly murdered their prophet son, Zechariah, who dared to challenge the king's idolatrous ways. At first glance this looks like an example of the basest ingratitude.

54

How could he do it? How can we explain his sudden change of character and behavior after the death of his elderly counselor?

We need to remember the general moral deterioration of the times. We usually think of the period of the judges as the dark ages of Israel's history when "every man did that which was right in his own eyes." But was even that dark era worse than that of Joash? Jehoram, his grandfather, began his own reign by forthrightly killing all of his brothers. Athaliah, his grandmother, had deliberately tried to eliminate all claimants to the throne by stamping out the entire royal line.

Pagan idolatry was flourishing on every hand. Despite the efforts of some relatively good men such as Jehoiada, there is evidence of a strange lethargy and self-interest, even among the priests and Levites. In such a time of moral decline, when cruelty and brutality seemed to be the "normal" pattern, human life seemed cheap and compassion unrealistic. In such an era, there is likely to be a tendency to adopt an expedient, hedonistic attitude. Since life is insecure and uncertain, there is a strong urge to get what you can out of life by whatever means are at hand. Certainly the general moral climate of the times was not such as would have promoted human understanding, sympathy, and appreciation. Joash was a product of very troubled times.

We need to keep in mind also the unnatural childhood of the boy king. Rescued from the fury of his diabolical grandmother, he was reared for six years in secrecy. There was always the threat of possible discovery as the wicked Athaliah and her gestapo created a reign of suspicion and terror in the land.

It is really amazing that a healthy, lively, noisy little boy could have been successfully concealed under such circumstances. Isn't it incredible that someone didn't reveal his presence to one of Athaliah's secret agents? In any event, his childhood must have been an unnatural one, hardly designed to prepare him for the rough and tough game of politics and intrigue which surrounded and permeated the life of the court.

This leads to a third factor which probably, more than any other, accounts for the behavior of Joash: He probably was unnaturally dominated by his mentor, Jehoiada. The latter was fundamentally a good man with healthy motivations. He and his wife rescued Joash, reared him, and arranged for his elevation to the throne. Later on, Jehoiada found two wives for him. Through the years he stood by the young king's side, possibly overshadowing or even dominating him more than either of them consciously realized.

To Jehoiada, now over 100 years of age, Joash was probably always the "little boy" who needed his protection and advice. Perhaps Jehoiada never really "took his hands off," as wise parents or guardians deliberately plan to do as their children enter adolescence and approach adulthood. We often think of such "smother love" as a particular hazard of mothers. And, indeed, it often is. The ultimate and crucial test of healthy mother love is precisely this: Will she deliberately and joyfully plan for and encourage the full psychological independence of her child? Will two who were once one become two genuinely independent persons? But this is a problem for many fathers, too! It is very easy for the father or the mother to rationalize, to find the "best" reasons for keeping their hands on their children when the latter ought to be truly "on their own."

The fact that Jehoiada chose the wives of Joash may be significant. Of course, it may have been the usual practice then for parents, or parent substitutes, to choose their children's mates. But one wonders!

The fact is that, just as soon as Jehoiada died, a drastic change occurred in the behavior of Joash. This does not speak well of the kind of training the older man had given

56

the erstwhile boy-king. Something must have been lacking. Had the older man actually put the younger on his own? Had Joash learned to make responsible, adult choices? Had he learned to think for himself? Had he learned to gather facts, organize them, weigh alternatives, and make rational, discriminating personal decisions?

The possibility that Jehoiada had dominated Joash may help to explain the latter's violent, irrational reaction to the rebuke of Zechariah, Jehoiada's son.

When Jehoiada died, the attitude of Joash may well have been: Now that the old man is gone, I'm really going to be king—in fact, as well as in name! This attitude may, indeed, have made him more vulnerable to the obsequious approach of the princes of Judah. Then when Zechariah, who reminded the king of his indebtedness and close relationship to Jehoiada, took a public stand against the king and his new policies, the reaction was violent and irrational: Away with him; let him be stoned to death!

To the complex relationship between Jehoiada and Joash must be added another subtle element. One of the major aims of Joash as king was the restoration of the Temple and the purification of the worship of the God of Israel. He seems to have been very sincere and earnest about this. But there was a strange reluctance on the part of Jehoiada and other religious leaders to "get going" on the project. In fact, 23 years passed without any significant action being taken in the restoration of the Temple. The priests and Levites seemed to be content to take the revenues for themselves. This irritated the king and he called Jehoiada to account for the apparent lethargy and delay (II Chron. 24:4-6). The suggestion is that Jehoiada and the other religious leaders had strong vested interests and were content to let the Temple remain in disrepair, as long as they were secure in their privileges. Perhaps to this should be added the observations of the historian in II Kings 12:3, "But the high places were not taken away: the people still sacrificed and burnt incense in the high places." In other words, Jehoiada was willing to settle for something less than a complete religious and spiritual reformation. Joash was perhaps led to the conclusion that some kind of working compromise with idolatry and evil was inevitable after all. Jehoiada had set the pattern.

While all of the foregoing, and other hereditary, environmental, and personal influences, may have played a part in the strange behavior of Joash, there is still the central factor of his own sinful heart. Despite a general low level of moral and spiritual life, a hazardous and inadequate series of childhood experiences, and the loss of his aged counselor, he could have been an upright, honorable, godly king if he had chosen to be that kind. But he lifted himself up in pride and self-will, and in spite of training and the counsel of many prophets of God, he chose to turn from the pathway of righteousness to pagan idolatry.

His proud heart of unbelief was nourished by the obeisance of the ungodly princes of Judah. He was determined to go his own way despite repeated warnings of the prophets of the Most High.

No doubt Joash and Zechariah had grown up together. They may have been close personal friends. If anyone had suggested that someday Joash would have ordered the murder of his friend, he would have been laughed to scorn. But such is the deceptiveness of sin. No man knows what he may eventually do when he leaves the pathway of rectitude, and takes the road leading from God and holiness.

The prophet Jeremiah declared that "the heart is deceitful above all things, and desperately wicked: who can know it?" (Jer. 17:9) Joash was no exception. The only safety for any of us is found in the redemptive work of our Lord Jesus Christ on Calvary's cross. He alone can solve the problem of sin in human personality. Only in a constant dependence on the merits of His atoning blood and the guidance and empowerment of His indwelling Spirit is there hope and safety for any man.

The story of Joash is, in many respects, a tragedy. We cannot help but think "what might have been." He might have gone down in Judah's history as one of its most noble, exemplary, useful, and godly kings. But, severely wounded in a battle which by all odds he should have won, except for the judgment of God, he was murdered in his own bed. His own servants conspired against him "because of the blood of the son of Jehoiada the priest." And they did not even give him the honor of being buried in the tombs of the kings.

The Word of God declares that the experiences of the children of Israel were preserved as examples, and "they are written for our admonition, upon whom the ends of the world are come" (I Cor. 10:11). And the Apostle Paul's conclusion is, "Wherefore let him that thinketh he standeth take heed lest he fall. There hath no temptation taken you but such as is common to man: but God is faithful, who will not suffer you to be tempted above that ye are able; but will with the temptation also make a way to escape, that ye may be able to bear it. Wherefore, my dearly beloved, flee from idolatry" (I Cor. 10:12-14).

7

ESTHER:
Putting Your Life on the Line

Esther, queen of the Medo-Persian Empire, uttered one of the most dramatic statements ever heard when she said, "So will I go in unto the king, which is not according to the law: and if I perish, I perish" (Esther 4:16). These words represent a "gamble," a calculated risk, which involved her very life. In her own mind, she had, in advance, paid the "last full measure of devotion" for her daring venture. She literally "took her life in her hands."

The background for Esther's act of superlative courage is found in the book of the Bible which bears her name. The story opens with the introduction of Ahasuerus, ruler of the great Medo-Persian Empire. He was the son of the famed Persian military leader Xerxes. Ahasuerus had had to face considerable opposition in making good his claim to his father's throne. Rebel armies were led by his father's brother, Artabanus; and by his own brother, Hystapes. But at the end of three years of bloody civil war, Ahasuerus had put down all major opposition and established his absolute control over the vast Persian Empire of 120 provinces extending from Ethiopia to India.

Secure on the throne, in his palace in Shushan (Susa), he decided that the time had arrived for an appropriate victory celebration. Thus for 180 days he lavishly entertained the military and civil leaders of the empire. Then for seven days he staged a celebration for the people of the capital city. All local citizens were invited to the week-long feast in the gorgeous, many-hued palace. The wine flowed freely and the emperor generously paid the bill.

Vashti, the queen of Ahasuerus, a noble and beautiful woman, also joined in the festivities. She too gave a lavish banquet for the women of the court in her royal quarters.

On the seventh day of the king's celebration he hit on the idea of crowning the festivities by presenting his beautiful queen to the gala and riotous throng of drinking and drunken merrymakers. But the king's judgment and perhaps his memory were dulled and disrupted by the excessive concentration of alcohol in his blood. Queen Vashti, with a dignity and nobility of character befitting her high position, refused to come and be made a spectacle for the pleasure of the dissolute throng. She was not only "fair to behold," but was also a remarkable woman of unusual virtue and sterling character.

Ahasuerus, having so recently climbed to the pinnacle of his power, was enraged at the independent, courageous behavior of Vashti. "His anger burned within him."

Faced with such an unusual display of feminine independence, the king turned to his seven key advisers. One of these, Memucan by name, seems also to have had a wife of some strength of character. He too felt insecure. He argued before the king and the assembled princes:

"Not only to the king has Queen Vashti done wrong, but also to all the princes and all the peoples who are in all the provinces of King Ahasuerus. For this deed of the queen will be made known to all women, causing them to look with contempt upon their husbands, since they will say, 'King Ahasuerus commanded Queen Vashti to be brought before him, and she did not come.' This very day the ladies of Persia and Media who have heard of the queen's behavior will be telling it to all the king's princes, and there will be contempt and wrath in plenty. If it please the king, let a royal order go forth from him, and let it be written among the laws of the Persians and the Medes so that it may not be altered, that Vashti is to come no more before King Ahasuerus; and let the king give her royal position to another who is better than she. So when the decree made by the king is proclaimed through-out all his kingdom, vast as it is, all women will give honor to their husbands, high and low" (Esther 1:16-20, RSV).

This shrewd advice pleased the king and the princes, all of whom must have been living in fear that their wives might now openly dominate them. So letters were dispatched to all provinces and in all the various dialects to the effect that "every man should bear rule in his own house." So a crisis situation, involving a great threat to male dominance, was presumably resolved. What a stroke of masculine genius!

One wonders just what went through the mind of Ahasuerus when he had calmed down. "He remembered Vashti, and what she had done, and what was decreed against her." He probably also remembered her nobility of character, and beauty of face and figure. And he may have secretly cursed himself for his stupidity. But the law of the Medes and Persians could not be changed. So, what had been done had been done. What next?

His servants soon had an attractive suggestion. Why not stage the first "Miss Universe" contest and find the king a new wife, and perhaps a dozen comely concubines? The idea seemed good to Ahasuerus. So officers were appointed to gather the most beautiful young women from throughout the realm. In Shushan, the young women were each given a full year's preparation before their presentation to the king. First prize in the pageant was nothing less than becoming queen of the empire as successor to the noble, but unfortunate, Vashti.

Among the leading candidates in this first notable beauty contest was Hadasseh, better known as Esther. She was a lovely and talented Jewish girl whose father and mother were both deceased. She had been reared by her uncle, Mordecai, an attendant at the king's court. Esther quickly earned the goodwill and special favor of Hegai, who was placed in charge of the beautiful candidates. He gave her seven attendants, and one of the best apartments in the king's harem. Esther also won the good favor of all others who came in contact with her.

She was not only beautiful to behold, but had qualities of graciousness and nobility of character which made her a strong candidate for the queen's crown. King Ahasuerus was equally impressed with the personal qualities and charm of the dark-eyed beauty whose Jewish origin was unknown to him.

> The king loved Esther more than all the women, and she found grace and favor in his sight more than all the virgins, so that he set the royal crown on her head and made her queen instead of Vashti. Then the king gave a great banquet to all his princes and servants; it was Esther's banquet (Esther 2:17-18, RSV).

The drama of the career of Esther now enters a new phase and the villain of the story comes onto the stage. He was an ambitious, ruthless man named Haman. The king was impressed by him, and he was quickly promoted to a position of great authority over all the princes. The royal command was that all the court personnel should bow to Haman, showing proper respect. But there was one of the king's servants who refused to bow and thereby render the

63

expected reverence. This was Mordecai, Queen Esther's uncle, and foster father. Apparently Mordecai felt that such deference to the wicked Haman would amount to the sin of idolatry, which was strictly forbidden by the law of God. Haman was also an Amalekite, the traditional enemies of the Jews whom God had commanded King Saul to "utterly destroy."

When Haman's attention was called to Mordecai's refusal to bow, he reacted with the typical resentment of a small man who had been recently elevated to a position of undeserved eminence. The promotion had gone to his head. He was a bit dizzy with the height, and had an exaggerated sense of his own importance.

But it seemed irrational for such a big official to attack only one man, especially when he was only a lowly, Jewish palace guard! So Haman decided on a bigger project, more in keeping with what he considered his proper status and importance. He reasoned: Why not destroy all the Jews in the empire, and confiscate their property? This would not only give him sweet revenge for Mordecai's impertinent stubbornness, but it would be financially profitable to both himself and the empire!

So Haman cast lots, as was his custom, in order to determine the "lucky day" for his venture. Then he made his proposal to the naive Ahasuerus. It was as follows:

> "There is a certain people scattered abroad and dispersed among the peoples in all the provinces of your kingdom; their laws are different from those of every other people, and they do not keep the king's laws, so that it is not for the king's profit to tolerate them. If it please the king, let it be decreed that they be destroyed, and I will pay ten thousand talents of silver into the hands of those who have charge of the king's business, that they may put it into the king's treasuries" (Esther 3:8-9, RSV).

At this time, remember, Ahasuerus was totally unaware of the Jewish background of Queen Esther, and of her relationship to Mordecai.

Haman's diabolical proposal to liquidate all the Jews in the empire and confiscate their property sounded good to the unsuspecting and unscrupulous Ahasuerus. So he gave his approval and signet ring to Haman. The later acted with unusual dispatch and an edict was quickly prepared: "to destroy, to slay, and to annihilate all Jews, young and old, women and children, in one day, the thirteenth day of the twelfth month, which is the month of Adar, and to plunder their goods" (3:13, RSV).

Copies of the edict were sent by special messengers throughout the empire. We read that "the king and Haman sat down to drink; but the city of Shushan was perplexed." It was a strange and alarming decree.

When Mordecai heard of the proposed program, he "rent his clothes, and put on sackcloth with ashes"—evidence of mourning—and went into the midst of Shushan, crying "with a loud and bitter cry." Then he came and stood before the king's gate. Likewise, in every province there was great mourning among the Jews with fasting, weeping, wailing, and the wearing of sackcloth and ashes.

Queen Esther was greatly distressed at Mordecai's behavior, and sent to discover its meaning and purpose. Mordecai then reported all the facts and sent a copy of the king's decree to her. He also urged her strongly to go to the king and plead with him for the lives of her people.

Esther's reply to Mordecai called attention to an imperial custom which would make it almost impossible to even to talk to the king: "If any man or woman goes to the king inside the inner court without being called, there is but one law; all alike are to be put to death, except the one to whom the king holds out the golden scepter that he may live" (4:11, RSV).

Esther told Mordecai that she had not been called before the king for 30 days, but Mordecai's response was immediate and to the point:

> "Think not that in the king's palace you will escape
> any more than all the other Jews. For if you keep silence
> at such a time as this, relief and deliverance will rise for
> the Jews from another quarter, but you and your father's
> house will perish. And who knows whether you have not
> come to the kingdom for such a time as this?" (4:13-14,
> RSV)

Esther's reply is one of the most eloquent, moving, and
heroic statements of all time.

> "Go, gather all the Jews to be found in Susa, and hold
> a fast on my behalf, and neither eat nor drink for three
> days, night or day. I and my maids will also fast as you
> do. Then I will go to the king, though it is against the
> law; and if I perish, I perish" (4:16, RSV).

Esther's deliberate decision to enter the king's presence
unbidden, although legally this was a crime involving the
death penalty, was a calculated risk. The usual way of de-
scribing such behavior is to call it a gamble. But was it?
What are the differences, if any, between gambling and taking calculated risks? Is life itself, as some say, a gamble?

The fact is that there is a very fundamental difference
between a gamble and a calculated risk. The most important
factor in a gamble is chance. Gambling exists when one
person, on the basis of chance, risks a value and loses, while
another person, on the basis of chance, risks a value, and
wins. Nothing of intrinsic worth (other than "fun") is
manufactured, created, transported, or exchanged. Sometimes, of course, the odds against winning are less than
chance. A person playing a "one-armed bandit" slot
machine should know that he cannot possibly win in the
long run. The designer of the machine has set it mechanical-
ly so that the odds over a period of time are clearly against
the player and in favor of the owner of the machine.

Gambling is one of the most serious psychological,
moral, and economic illnesses of our day. More than $20
billion is spent on gambling each year, and the amount is
rapidly growing. Recently several states have legalized

lotteries to supplement tax revenues. The underworld and syndicated crime are deeply entrenched in gambling activities.

Why do people gamble? The motives are many and varied, although all of them express the universal and normal urge to self-transcendence. The latter involves the desire to expand one's experiences, relieve the dullness and routineness of life, and escape from the irritations and frustrations of daily living.

The gambler "gets away from it all" for a brief time. He is emotionally and personally involved in what he is doing, even though his involvement may be only with a machine. His sated or exhausted emotions are pepped up or aroused by the thrill of winning or the disappointment of losing. For a time he is able to forget the nagging worry of a deteriorating marriage, a business which may be going on the "rocks," the pangs of unrelieved guilt, or the anxiety of an uncertain future. He is seeking for life in a larger dimension —for life with a capital *L*.

For a brief time he seeks to transcend his encapsulated self. Of course, if he is asked why he gambles, he will give more specific reasons. Oddly, some gamblers actually desire to lose. They punish themselves by losing, and thus atone for feelings of guilt. They play on and on until they at last exhaust their resources. Their compulsive behavior occasionally amazes even hardened professional operators.

The enthralled gambler is usually oblivious of time as well as of family or business responsibilities and obligations. He is not a spectator in the "game"; he is a living participant. This explains the fascination and the great hazard of gambling. For many persons, it is as much a compulsive disease as alcoholism. There is a strange, mystical quality about the activity. Gamblers are likely to be confirmed optimists, no matter how frequently and consistently they lose. They may know that the honest odds (not to say the "fix") are stacked against them, yet they are absolutely

67

convinced that someday luck will be on their side, and they will win a fortune.

Gambling, like all of Satan's devices, represents a perversion of a legitimate, God-given urge. The devil never builds any roads. In this instance, the urge is, as previously stated, that of self-transcendence: to live fully, freely, excitingly. And the particular form that this general life-force takes is the urge to take a calculated risk. A provocative Christian thinker has suggested that "God doesn't have any use for a person who won't take a chance." That may be questioned but it is certainly true that the capacity to think things through, weigh all available evidence, and make a discriminating, rational decision at the strategic and appropriate time is a mark of a healthy, grown-up personality.

To make a discriminating decision and then accept the consequences "in stride" whether they are good, bad, or indifferent is evidence of personality maturity. It is also a key to success in every area of life. But it is not gambling. It is accepting the risks attached to every decision we must make.

Life is full of such calculated risks where we must make our choice without knowing with certainty in advance how everything will turn out. Think of the risks involved in choosing a mate and promising to love, honor, and sustain him or her in sickness and in health, for better or for worse, until parted by death! That's a calculated risk for you! Think of the hazards involved in begetting a child. Something might happen in development and he may be born crippled in body or mind. When he becomes an adult he may become a criminal and bring sorrow or disgrace to his parents. Think of the business investments, often involving millions of dollars, which are based, to some degree, on faith in the nation's future prosperity, and the integrity of the promises made by associates.

Children need to be given training in the art of taking calculated risks. They must learn to gather facts, organize them, figure out the pros and the cons, make clear-cut decisions when the time is ripe, and courageously accept the consequences whether they are favorable or unfavorable.

The ability, willingness, and capacity to know when to take a calculated risk adds zest and an element of healthy adventuresomeness to life. This capacity enables a person to avoid the debilitating consequence of habitual indecisiveness, and that "old tired feeling" which accompanies this neurotic and unhealthy life-style.

Properly defined, the acceptance of the way of Jesus, the Christian faith, is life's supreme calculated risk. Such a master choice is in no sense irrational. It is based on evidence, but it goes beyond the intellect and involves man's total personality, including the will. The Christian faith, in its very nature, transcends mere facts and ventures. It is based on the reality and dependability of the unseen God revealed in and through His Son, the Lord Jesus Christ. The evidences for its validity are not merely historic as revealed in the Word of God, but are progressively validated as His way is discovered to work out in personal experience and in human relationships. Yet faith is never coercive. The evidence is never so complete as to be intellectually compelling. There is always a personal "leap" in faith. It involves a total risking of one's very life and destiny on the revelation of God in Christ.

Was the venture of Esther such a healthy, calculated risk? Indeed it was! Her decision to go unbidden into the presence of Ahasuerus was not just a gamble. She knew the king. She knew that he loved and admired her. Although she had not been called into his presence for a period of 30 days, she may have known of extenuating circumstances. At the same time, she was aware of the fickleness of an Oriental despot. She remembered the noble and lovely Vashti, and her undeserved fate.

On the other hand, there was the dire threat to her own people. She knew Haman all too well: his pompous pride, his base cruelty, his madness for power, his hatred for the Jews.

Then there was her awareness of divine resources: the power of fasting, and the importance of prayer. She was thoroughly convinced that the God of Israel had indeed brought her to the kingdom for just such a time as this.

So Esther carefully and critically weighed all these factors and made her decision: she would take the calculated risk of entering the presence of Ahasuerus unbidden, and "if I perish, I perish."

As it turned out, her risk "paid off." Her venture was successful. Haman was hanged on the very gallows he had prepared for Mordecai, and the latter was elevated by Ahasuerus to a position of great power and influence. Best of all, Esther's people were saved and their condition in the empire was even more favorable than before the crisis.

Queen Esther came to her great moment of influence by divine appointment. Through the counsel of Mordecai she recognized her hour of destiny and through prayer and fasting she was prepared to follow through. She took the necessary calculated risk which enabled the sovereign God to use her in a momentous way.

Crucial occasions of testing and moral decision confront each of us from time to time. Let us earnestly seek the guidance of the Spirit of Truth that we may have the judgment to recognize our moments of high destiny, and then act with intelligence and courage in line with the sovereign purposes of Almighty God. In some sense, then, we shall realize, like Queen Esther, that we have "come to the kingdom for such a time as this."

8

JOB:
Meeting the Challenge
of Unrelieved Stress

Job lived many centuries ago in what is now Saudi Arabia. He was faced with so much psychological and moral stress that his name is almost synonymous with trouble. The account of his life is found in one of the oldest divisions of the Old Testament. The Book of Job is actually a great epic. It is a poetic drama in three acts, with a prose introduction and a prose conclusion. The circumstances leading to Job's extraordinary trial are given in the introduction.

Job was an exceptionally good man, for his day, or for any other. He was blameless and upright. He was one who feared God, and turned away from evil. He was also a very wealthy man—in lands, livestock, friends, and family. As is the custom with many large families today, Job and his family had many enjoyable social times together. In fact, they had a regular succession of dinner dates. In the midst of this social whirl, Job was greatly concerned about the spiritual welfare of his seven sons and three daughters. So he offered regular morning prayers and sacrifices for each. This he did continually.

With this scene of family prosperity and happiness as a background, we are told that on a certain day the "sons of God" came to present themselves before the Lord, and Satan, the evil one or adversary, came also. Of him, the Lord God inquired: "Hast thou considered my servant Job, that there is none like him in the earth?" Satan's immediate and cynical response was, "Doth Job fear God for nought? . . . put forth thine hand now, and touch all that he hath, and he will curse thee to thy face."

But the Lord God was convinced of Job's unselfish devotion and enduring fidelity. So Satan was given permission to touch Job's possessions. There was, however, a divine limitation: "Upon himself put not forth thine hand."

Consequently Job was suddenly confronted with a series of devastating, anxiety-producing losses. In rapid-fire succession they came:

> The Sabeans fell upon and carried away his 500 yoke of oxen and 500 she-asses;
>
> Lightning struck down his 7,000 sheep;
>
> The Chaldeans carried away his 3,000 camels;
>
> And, as a final and awful climax to the day's incredible losses, a cyclonic wind struck the house where Job's 10 children were drinking wine, and all were killed without warning.

This shocking combination of natural and moral evil, and the cumulative buildup of psychological and moral stress would have brought a man of limited spiritual and personality reserves to the breaking point. Not so with Job. He "arose, and rent his mantle, and shaved his head, and fell down upon the ground, and worshipped."

The dramatic scene shifts again and the Lord and

Satan resume their conversation about Job. Satan is reminded again of Job's blameless and upright life, and the fact that he still "holdeth fast his integrity, although thou movedst me against him, to destroy him without cause." Satan's arrogant rejoinder was: "Skin for skin, yea, all that a man hath will he give for his life. But put forth thine hand now, and touch his bone and his flesh, and he will curse thee to thy face." The Lord's response was: "Behold, he is in thine hand; but save his life."

Job was now smitten with "sore boils from the sole of his foot unto his crown." Evidence indicates that this was black leprosy or elephantiasis. This is a terrible and painful disease in which hands and feet swell to enormous proportions, the skin cracks, and putrefying sores break out. In that ancient day, black leprosy was looked upon as the special curse of God upon the worst of sinners.

Job was now isolated and sat on an ash heap outside the village wall. Here he scraped his sores with bits of pottery and bemoaned the day of his birth.

To add to his catastrophic misfortunes his wife now said, "Dost thou still retain thine integrity? curse God, and die." But Job's instant rejoinder was, "Thou speakest as one of the foolish women speaketh." "In all this did not Job sin with his lips."

Then it was that Job's three "friends" or "comforters" appeared on the scene. So overwhelmed were they by his unhappy state and altered appearance that for seven days and nights not one word was spoken. But their silence was hardly the result of "sympathy through empathy"; for when they finally spoke, their persistent endeavor was an effort to convince Job of sins which he had not committed.

These speeches and Job's replies constitute the main body of the great epic drama. At length, God himself spoke out of the whirlwind, and all voices, including the rather belligerent voice of Job, were silenced in awe and humility.

At the outset of the first speech by Eliphaz, the Temanite, oldest of Job's "friends," a wonderful compliment is given to Job. Here it is as translated by Dr. James Moffatt: "You have yourself set many right, and put strength into feeble souls; your words have kept men on their feet, the weak-kneed you have nerved" (Job 4:3-4).

How could Job's words have "kept men on their feet"? On first thought, words—anyone's words—seem weak and fragile. Yet a word is an attempt to communicate an idea, a truth, a conviction. Surely words which communicate great truths do have upholding power. They do keep men on their feet. They are, as Solomon said, "like apples of gold in pictures of silver." Yes, genuine convictions, meaningful insights, great truths do keep men on their feet in the midst of life's severest tests and most stringent trials.

Carl Jung, one of the world's greatest authorities on personality problems, often spoke of the aimlessness, rootlessness, and purposelessness which characterize so many lives today. He called this aimlessness the "existential neurosis of our times." In order for life to be lived greatly and triumphantly, says Jung, there must be great purposes, meaningful goals, sustaining values, a truly satisfying philosophy of life.

A good question, then, is this: What were the words of Job that had inspired men and which now sustained Job himself in his fiery trial? These may well be words which will keep each of us "on our feet" in life's testing hours.

The first sustaining conviction of Job was his determination to maintain his moral integrity. He refused to admit personal, conscious guilt when none existed. He steadfastly refused to agree with his accusers who argued that his misfortunes must be the result of his personal sins. He persistently maintained "a conscience void of offence toward God, and toward men."

With possessions and children swept away, "Job sinned not, nor charged God foolishly." When his health had vanished and his wife had turned against him, Job held steady. Pressed almost beyond measure by the false accusations of his so-called friends, he declared, "My lips shall not speak wickedness, nor my tongue utter deceit. . . . till I die I will not remove mine integrity from me. My righteousness I hold fast." He declared that he esteemed the word of God more than his necessary food, and held firmly to the propositions that "the fear of the Lord, that is wisdom; and to depart from evil is understanding."

A guilt-free, Spirit-quickened, Bible-informed, exercised conscience is one of the greatest assets anyone can possess from the standpoint of physical, mental, emotional, and spiritual health. Hardly anything is more important in a healthy personality. Such a conscience is a major support in every trying experience.

Through repentance and faith in the Lord Jesus Christ, guilt is remitted and the believer stands justified in the sight of a holy God. Through the atoning merit of the Saviour, the conscience may be purged, and one may accept himself, because he is "accepted in the beloved." Through the great ethical principles of the Scriptures, and the guidance of the Holy Spirit, the conscience may be developed, matured, and kept free of guilt complexes.

Thus by God's power and grace, revealed in and through our Lord Jesus Christ, and the guidance of the Holy Spirit and the Word of God, a person may maintain his moral integrity—a conscience void of offense toward God and man. Here indeed is a "word" that keeps redeemed men on their feet.

The second great healthy insight in the thought of Job which sustained him in the midst of apparent disaster was his declaration of a humble, teachable attitude. "Teach me," he said, "and I will hold my tongue: and cause me to understand wherein I have erred." And, then, when God had spoken out of the whirlwind, Job confessed: "I uttered that I understood not; things too wonderful for me, which I knew not. . . . but now mine eye seeth thee. Wherefore I abhor myself, and repent in dust and ashes."

Humility and teachability are inseparable companions. And both are marks of a truly secure and mature Christian personality. Such flexibility and adaptability are in no sense incompatible with great moral convictions for which one is prepared to die—or live! In fact, both of these—adaptability and strong convictions—are characteristics of the ideal Christian person.

In contrast to the humility and teachability of the mature Christian is the rigid behavior of the immature and insecure person—even in matters of little or no consequence. Such persons have personality structures comparable to cast iron, rather than tough, resilient, high-tension steel. Consequently, the "cast iron" structure, devoid of "flexible strength," shatters when the pressures of life reach a critical breaking point.

But Job, humble and teachable, looked upon his baffling, testing experience as an opportunity to learn. This attitude was a word which kept him on his feet as the hopes and dreams of a lifetime disappeared in a single day.

The third great conviction that kept Job on his feet was his quiet confidence in the character of God as good and just. Note his remarks: "The Lord gave, and the Lord hath taken away"—"Shall we receive good at the hand of God, and shall we not receive evil?"—"He knoweth the way that I take"—"I have esteemed the words of his mouth more than my necessary food"—"Though he slay me, yet will I trust in him . . . He also shall be my salvation."

And when God finally revealed himself out of the whirlwind, He did not give Job a *rational* explanation of his dire situation. No, He gave Job what he really needed most—a more adequate revelation of himself: His power, majesty, greatness, and goodness. This fuller revelation of

God himself was Job's greatest need—and ours! With all of us, our God is too small.

Many, perhaps most, of the problems of our lives will not be fully understood, here and now. But we need not be overwhelmed by these baffling mysteries. Not if our conception of God is adequate.

The word "Comforter," used by Jesus in referring to the Holy Spirit, suggests that He strengthens the believer, not by what He gives, but simply by His personal and intimate presence.

Clyde Yarbrough tells of an incident of his boyhood. He and his father were caught in a sudden storm while hunting. Unable to return home because of the rising streams, they found shelter from the cold and rain in a little cabin in the woods. In the midst of the raging storm, cold and shivering from the rain, Clyde tells of snuggling up close to his big, strong father and placing his shivering, little hand in the big, strong hand of his father. And when he did, the "beetles of fear" were driven from his childish mind. Years later, remembering this incident, he wrote:

> I do not ask that my path be plain,
>   And all its pitfalls clear—
> Steady, I can walk in the blinding rain
>   If only Thou art near.
>
> I do not seek for release from pain,
>   Nor from life's tasks austere—
> All that comes I can turn to gain
>   If only Thou art near.
>
> I do not beg for the easy load,
>   Nor freedom from strain or fear—
> With courage strong I can face life's road
>   If only Thou art near.
>
> I do not plead for burdens light,
>   But for faith to persevere—

> *I willingly toil with all my might*
> *If only Thou art near.* *

The fourth great sustaining word of Job was prophetic: his poignant recognition of the imperative need of a mediator between God and man. He pleads for a "daysman"— one who could lay one hand upon God and the other on himself, and mediate between them. "I know," he said, "that it is so of a truth: but how should a man be just with God? If he will contend with him, he cannot answer him one of a thousand. . . . For he is not a man, as I am, that . . . we should come together in judgment. Neither is there any daysman betwixt us, that might lay his hand upon us both."

Here Job refers to a familiar custom of that ancient time. One of the elders of the village would sit in the gate as a daysman or judge. In case of some dispute between neighbors, the daysman would lay one hand on each of the disputants and mediate or resolve the controversy. So Job desperately pleads for a mediator between God and himself.

We are more fortunate than Job. For we do have such a Daysman. He is the Lord Jesus Christ, Mediator between God and man. He is our great High Priest, both *merciful* and *faithful*. As the Son of Man, He understands all our trials and tests, for He personally experienced them. He was tempted in all points as we are, yet without sin. He is therefore full of compassion, sympathy, understanding. Like the high priest of old, He wears the name of every believer on His breastplate, close to His heart. He cares.

But our great High Priest, the unique God-man, is also the Eternal Son of God, Creator and Sustainer of the vast universe in which we live. Thus He is faithful, well able to do all that He has promised! We are therefore invited to come boldly to His throne of grace and find help in every

---

*R. C. Yarbrough, *Triumphant Personality* (New York: Macmillan, 1949), p. 24. Used by permission.

time of need. Again, like the high priest of old, He wears the name of every believer on His shoulder—the symbol of strength.

Job's unwavering faith in the immortality of man was another upholding word that kept him on his feet. His statements of faith in immortality are all the more remarkable because the theme is often obscure in the Old Testament. Recall his classic words: "For I know that my redeemer liveth, and that he shall stand at the latter day upon the earth: and though after my skin worms destroy this body, yet in my flesh shall I see God: whom I shall see for myself, and mine eyes shall behold, and not another; though my reins be consumed within me."

On occasion, each of us should face up to the simple, irreducible, ultimate facts of life. One of these is this: Man is mortal or he is immortal. No other alternative is possible. The Scriptures teach, and we confidently declare, that all of us, while having our beginnings in time, will exist somewhere as living, conscious beings *forever!* And this fact makes all the difference, here and now.

If man is mortal, and this life ends it all, then the only wise course is to have maximum enjoyment as long as possible. But if man is immortal—and he is—then this life becomes a preparation for the unending ages yet to be.

It was said that Socrates, having been condemned to die, was urged by his friends to violate what he thought to be his personal integrity on the grounds that he would likely live for 10 more years. With blazing eyes, the wise old philosopher is supposed to have exclaimed: "What are 10 years for a man who expects to live forever!" Exactly!

One of the finest statements by the late Dr. James B. Chapman reflects the perspective which a firm faith in immortality gives to a thoughtful person. "Since God is eternal and I am immortal, I can wait. If others are chosen in the current elections, there is still plenty of time for me.

If others push in ahead and get their hire, I can wait until my inheritance is given. *There are too many tomorrows for me to accept as final any slight or failure or defeat that may come today"* (italics mine).

But, one might ask, does such a conviction of man's immortality keep Christian men on their feet in our day? One evening Wilfred Grenfell, Christian missionary doctor, found himself on an ice floe drifting slowly out into the North Atlantic. He spent a desperate night. To avoid being frozen to death, he killed several of his dogs and wrapped their furs about him. The next morning he tied several frozen dog legs together and made a crude flag, hoping to attract attention. At length he was rescued, snow-blinded, with hands and feet frozen. Listen to this testimony at the close of his arduous ordeal:

> I can honestly say that from first to last not a single sensation of fear crossed my mind. My own faith in the mystery of immortality is so untroubled that it seemed almost natural to be passing to the portal of death from an ice floe. Quite unbidden, the words of the old hymn kept running through my mind:
>
> > *My God, my Father, while I stray*
> > *Far from home on life's rough way,*
> > *Oh, teach me from my heart to say,*
> > *"Thy will be done."*

Yes, a conviction of man's immortality is a word that keeps men of faith on their feet today—even as in ages past.

Job's final word was not so much a spoken word as a lived-out word. It was a definitive, conclusive answer to Satan's cynical question: "Will a man serve God for nothing?" What a contemporary question that is! Is religion, after all, only a refined kind of selfishness? Does a man serve God for what he gets out of the relationship in terms of material gain, social prestige, or personal recognition? Or is there a service for God which is based on a complete, total, undivided love for God because God alone

80

is worthy of such unqualified love and unreserved devotion?

Job's lived-out answer for all time is: *Job serves God for nothing!* He serves and loves God for God's sake alone! His integrity is no vulgar, selfish barter! His fidelity to God is not based on reward. It is a heart loyalty, a hunger and thirsting for God himself—because He alone is utterly worthy. Such love and fidelity survive loss and heartache and chastisement. Such devotion reaches up out of the apparently contradictory circumstances of life, out of the darkness and hardness—as the needle seeks the pole—to the Life and the Light beyond. Job *does* serve God for nothing!

Such love and devotion to God for God's sake, because *He alone is worthy* of our total fidelity and undivided love, has upholding power beyond measure. It is a great word which has always kept wholly committed men on their feet no matter how trying the circumstances were.

These, then, are "words" that keep men on their feet:

1. A guilt-free, Spirit-cleansed, Bible-informed, exercised conscience, void of offense toward God and man.

2. A humble, teachable attitude that views every experience as an opportunity for God, to reveal His glory and guide the growth of His children.

3. A growing confidence in the greatness and goodness and love of God.

4. A continuing dependence on the Lord Jesus Christ, our Mediator and great High Priest.

5. An unwavering faith in the immortality of man.

6. A love and service for God—for God's sake alone.

These were convictions that kept Job on his feet. They are words that will sustain each of us today.

9

BATH-SHEBA:
Combining Adaptability
with Moral Strength

It was twilight on a sultry summer evening in the Middle East. A woman "very beautiful to look upon" had retired to the flat roof of her modest, Oriental-styled home. Surrounded by a parapet to shield her from any indiscreet prying eyes in the street below, she was taking advantage of the evening breeze. She was bathing.

Presumably unknown to her, a gifted, artistically inclined, passionate monarch was pacing about on the roof of his palace on a nearby elevation. It was David, the king, recently come to the throne of Israel. He was at home, resting from the uncertain and arduous conflicts which had marked his rise to power. His troops were still in the field, where perhaps, in all honor and integrity, he too, as their supreme commander, should have been.

Suddenly, through the gathering gloom, he saw the

naked and shapely woman. Immediately the hot passions of his tempestuous nature were aroused to fever pitch. He simply must have her! Every facet of his sensuous nature cried out in irrepressible hunger for her, and for satisfaction. And, after all, he *was* king! And who or what should deny him his will, and the satisfaction of his imperious libidinal urges?

Who was this woman with such unusual, attractive power? Inquiry revealed that she was the granddaughter of the king's wisest and most trusted counselor, Ahithophel. Bath-sheba was also the daughter of a member of the king's personal bodyguard, Eliam, one of the 37 captains of the nation's military forces. Not only so, but this woman who was so beautiful to behold was the faithful, and apparently recent, bride of another of the king's mighty warriors, Uriah the Hittite. Ahithophel, Eliam, Uriah—all were faithful, honorable, and trusted men whose loyalty to David and personal integrity had been proven again and again.

But all these and other considerations of friendship and loyalty and moral integrity were swept aside by the torrent of primitive, sexual passion which overwhelmed the king. The irrational urge to possess Bath-sheba banished all reason. Considerations of chivalry and morality were drowned in a flood of passion. Knowing full well who she was, "David sent messengers, and took her; and she came in unto him, and he lay with her; for she was purified from her uncleanness: and she returned unto her house" (II Sam. 11:4).

What was Bath-sheba's role in this adulterous affair? Did she protest violently to the messengers whom David sent to fetch her? Did she remind the king of his friendship with and indebtedness to her grandfather, her father, and her husband? Did she point out the king's moral responsibility to her faithful spouse, to the law of Moses, and to the Lord God of Israel?

We do not know the answer to these questions. If she did protest, it may have been halfhearted. After all, David *was* king, and the limits of royal powers were still largely undefined. It was an era of polygamous households and casual relationships. David was eventually to have at least nine wives and 10 concubines. And yet the stern rebuke of Nathan, God's faithful prophet, clearly indicates that David knew he was committing a dastardly sin in violation of God's law, and against Bath-sheba and Uriah.

Bath-sheba was doubtless an intelligent, as well as a very beautiful, woman. Her grandfather, Ahithophel, was best known for his extraordinary wisdom. His advice was compared to "an oracle of God." Bath-sheba's distinguished son, Solomon, is generally judged to have been one of the wisest of men.

But Bath-sheba's personality was not marked so much by her beauty of figure or intelligence as by her pliability. She seems to have been more flexible and spineless than she was wise or morally strong. As indicated, there is no sure evidence in the Scriptures that she was a *willing participant* in the adulterous affair with David. In fact, the parable told by God's faithful prophet, Nathan, when he confronted David with his sin puts the moral blame for the affair squarely on the king. But neither does the Sacred Record indicate any strong moral protest on the part of Bath-sheba.

The total impression of Bath-sheba's life is that she was almost always doing someone else's bidding. But in so doing she almost inevitably seemed to be achieving her own goals. Her personality is reflected in the simple but impressive way in which she announced to the king her (and *his*) predicament: "I am with child" (II Sam. 11:5). Those simple words were of enormous importance—even to a king! She didn't even bother to convey the message in person. Her words simply meant: "I am in trouble, and so are you! What are *you* going to do about *my* problem, and *yours?*"

The eleventh chapter of II Samuel is one of the saddest chapters in the entire Bible. It is a poignant and sobering illustration of the simple truth, "Be sure your sin will find you out." David, the man after God's own heart, tried unsuccessfully to cover up his illicit affair with Uriah's wife. Finally, in desperation, he ordered what amounted to the murder of Bath-sheba's faithful and valiant husband. At the same time the king put himself under terrible bondage to Joab, his coconspirator, and ruthless military commander. David finally attempted to cover up the whole sordid and sinful situation with a show of callous, nonchalant, pious cant.

The Scriptures declare that when Bath-sheba heard of her husband's death "she mourned for her husband." He had been a good man, a brave man, an honorable man. Although he was a foreigner, he had a greater sense of loyalty to David and to Israel than many an Israelite. In her more thoughtful moments, Bath-sheba must have indeed regretted the murder and loss of such an exemplary man.

The closing words of the story of this chapter in David's life are foreboding. "And when the mourning was past, David sent and fetched her to his house, and she became his wife, and bare him a son. But the thing that David had done displeased the Lord" (II Sam. 11:27).

God's displeasure was revealed in the dramatic confrontation between the prophet, Nathan, and the king (II Sam. 12:1-14). In Nathan's famous parable, Bath-sheba is portrayed as the "one little ewe lamb" of the poor man "which he had bought and nourished up: and it grew up together with him, and with his children; it did eat of his own meat, and drank of his own cup, and lay in his bosom, and was unto him as a daughter" (v. 3). In other words, the relationship between Bath-sheba and Uriah is described as exceptionally warm and close.

As a part of the penalty for this sad affair, the child—fruit of the adulterous relationship—died. And this occurred despite David's sincere repentance, and earnest, intercessory prayer (vv. 13-23).

The next child Bath-sheba bore was Solomon, who was destined to become successor to the throne. After the birth of Solomon, Bath-sheba disappeared for some time behind the curtains of David's harem. During the revolt of David's long-haired son, Absalom, David's family, other than his 10 concubines, accompanied him on his uncertain wanderings. It was during this chaotic period that Bath-sheba's wise and venerable grandfather, Ahithophel, committed suicide. The old man's confidence in and loyalty to David had apparently been irreparably shaken by the events surrounding David's relationship to Bath-sheba, and the murder of Uriah. Ahithophel had therefore joined with Absalom in his effort to seize the throne by force. However, when Absalom refused to follow Ahithophel's counsel, the old man, now completely convinced that Absalom's cause would fail, went home, put his affairs in order, and hanged himself (II Sam. 17:23). What thoughts went through Bath-sheba's mind when she heard of her beloved grandfather's tragic death, we can only guess.

Years passed and David became old and feeble. Solomon, son of Bath-sheba, was promised the throne of Israel by his father, who also commissioned him to build the Temple of God.

But Solomon's succession to the throne was not attained without a struggle. An older half brother, Adonijah, undertook to secure the throne for himself. Nathan, the prophet, heard of the plot, and immediately took decisive steps to thwart it. He persuaded Bath-sheba to intercede with the aged David on behalf of Solomon's claims to the throne. Her pleas with David were strategically reinforced by Nathan himself. David took immediate action. He re-assured Bath-sheba that their son, Solomon, would indeed be his successor. The result of David's prompt action was that the plot of Adonijah quickly collapsed. Solomon, now assured of the throne, granted a reprieve to Adonijah, conditioned upon the latter's continued loyalty and good behavior. The story is told in the first chapter of I Kings.

The reprieve did not last long. And in the ensuing events Bath-sheba was involved, pliantly as usual, in the affair. At the very end of David's life, a fair young virgin, Abishag, a Shunammite, had been added to his harem to care for the dying monarch. Now Adonijah sought Bath-sheba's aid in appealing to Solomon for permission for him, Adonijah, to marry Abishag.

Bath-sheba, apparently desiring to please everybody, and failing to see the implications of the matter, agreed to present the request to her son, King Solomon. The latter immediately interpreted the request as a renewal of the plot on the part of Adonijah to seize the throne by marrying the last of David's wives. Despite the fact that Solomon had promised the queen mother that her request on behalf of Adonijah would be honored, he refused to do so. In fact he assumed that Adonijah, by his action, had violated his "parole." So Adonijah was summarily executed.

Thus Bath-sheba, "the pliable one," passed from the scene. To the very end of her career she ran "true to form" —always carrying out the wishes of others. On the whole, with the exception of her last ill-advised action in behalf of Adonijah, she was usually successful; or more accurately, she helped others succeed in their ventures, whether good or bad. She was flexible, adaptable, pliable—to a fault. She seemed to possess flexibility without the accompanying moral strength which makes for strong character, personality health, and greatness in achievement.

Is it not possible that Solomon combined in his personality and character both the best and worst traits of his dynamic, tempestuous, artistic father and his sensuous, pliable mother? Despite a brilliant and spiritual beginning, the last half of his reign was a great tragedy. He became a driving, Oriental despot without a moral margin in his conduct. His policies actually planted the seeds for the dissolution of the kingdom under his foolish son, Rehoboam.

A bas-relief on the cathedral doors at Pisa, Italy, shows Solomon arising out of the grave on the day of judgment. He glances first to the right, at the righteous; then to the left, at the damned. He is apparently unsure as to which group he belongs to. And we wonder, too.

A phrase sometimes heard is "how to succeed without half trying." This seems to have been the story of Bathsheba's life. She usually got what she wanted. Yet she was more of a *reactor* than an *actor*. Divine providence, or the better judgment of others, often served to mitigate what might otherwise have been tragic consequences.

Adaptability, flexibility, pliability is a personality trait of value in human relationships. It is the antithesis of that rigid, compulsive behavior which is often so destructive of wholesome interpersonal relationships. Adaptability usually reflects a personal sense of security. An adaptable person is not driven to dominate or lean or isolate himself. He can be dominant or submissive, extroverted or introverted, active or passive—depending upon what is appropriate and fitting under the circumstances. He can lead, or follow. He can "fit in with others." He can gladly cooperate with the majority as long as no moral principles are violated.

But flexibility and adaptability must be balanced by strength in the healthy Christian personality. And strength involves having some overarching, personal moral convictions for which one is prepared to give his life.

One does not need to have a large number of such convictions. But such convictions must be absolutely basic. They must be carefully thought through. They must be one's very own. They must involve the great spiritual and

88

moral issues of life and destiny. There is no such thing as strong moral character, or great and significant living, without a few such convictions.

When such convictions are combined with flexibility and adaptability in human relationships—the result is an indispensable combination: *flexible strength.* This is what makes steel a basic component of all great structures which must stand the stresses of tempest and traffic. Great skyscrapers and bridges are designed to sway a certain amount but they always return to the original position. If they did not sway, they would break.

Is not this the lesson for living which we learn from the story of Bath-sheba, the Pliable? Just think! What a difference there would have been in her story—and David's and the history of Israel—if her moral strength had matched her pliability and her shapely beauty!

10

MANASSEH:
On Sowing Wild Oats

Both Israel and Judah had too many wicked rulers. But in the history of Judah there was one king whose name epitomizes the very worst in idolatrous and pagan practices. This was Manasseh. He was the son and successor of one of Judah's best kings, Hezekiah.

Was the birth of Manasseh an expression of the will of God? He was born three years after the Lord had said to his father, "Set thine house in order; for thou shalt die, and not live." But Hezekiah prayed desperately and insistently that his life might be extended. The result was something less than God's *intentional* will: a 15-year extension of his life. This period proved to be a disastrous one for both Hezekiah and his nation. It was during this period that Manasseh was born.

Why did Hezekiah pray so insistently? Perhaps one

reason was that he might have an heir to succeed him on the throne. How limited is the wisdom of man! For Manasseh was to undo virtually all that Hezekiah had been able to achieve in the way of moral and spiritual reform in Judah!

Contributing to and compounding the tragedy was the fact that Manasseh came to the throne while still a child of 12 years. His immaturity may have made him more vulnerable to the latent pagan influences which had survived his father's great reformation movement. To add to the evil, Manasseh reigned longer than any other king of Judah, a total of 55 years. In graphic detail, the Word of God describes the evil character of the first half of Manasseh's long reign:

> *And he did that which was evil in the sight of the Lord, after the abominations of the heathen, whom the Lord cast out before the children of Israel. For he built up again the high places which Hezekiah his father had destroyed; and he reared up altars for Baal, and made a grove, as did Ahab, king of Israel; and worshipped all the host of heaven, and served them. And he . . . used enchantments, and dealt with familiar spirits and wizards: he wrought much wickedness in the sight of the Lord, to provoke him to anger* (II Kings 21:2-6).
>
> *Manasseh seduced them to do more evil than did the nations whom the Lord destroyed before the children of Israel* (v. 9).
>
> *Moreover Manasseh shed innocent blood very much, till he had filled Jerusalem from one end to another; beside his sin wherewith he made Judah to sin, in doing that which was evil in the sight of the Lord* (v. 16).

The result of such a deliberate course of blatant evil was to invoke the judgment of God on the nation:

> *Therefore thus saith the Lord God of Israel, Behold, I am bringing such evil upon Jerusalem and Judah, that whosoever heareth of it, both his ears shall tingle. And I will stretch over Jerusalem the line of Samaria, and the plummet of the house of Ahab: and I will wipe Jerusalem as a man wipeth a dish, wiping it, and turning it upside*

down. And I will forsake the remnant of mine inheritance, and deliver them into the hand of their enemies; and they shall become a prey and a spoil to all their enemies (II Kings 21:12-14).

The cup of the wrath of God's judgment on Manasseh and Judah was full. The Lord was simply "fed up" with their idolatrous ways. So the prophet Jeremiah declared that even though God's special friends, Moses and Samuel, were to plead for divine mercy, it would be in vain. Judgment was at hand: "Wherefore the Lord brought upon them the captains of the host of the king of Assyria, which took Manasseh among the thorns, and bound him with fetters, and carried him to Babylon" (II Chron. 33:11).

This captivity was but the beginning of that dispersion of the people of Judah which would eventually scatter them among all nations. The word of the Lord was, "And I will cause them to be removed into all the kingdoms of the earth, *because of Manasseh* the son of Hezekiah king of Judah, for that which he did in Jerusalem" (Jer. 15:4, italics mine).

The Word of God thus declares that, in a special sense, Manasseh was responsible for destroying his nation. On his shoulders rested the prime cause for blasting the kingdom, and scattering God's chosen people. He was a kingdom wrecker. His influence, on balance, was evil and disastrous. Yet the strange and startling truth is that in his old age he was a good man; in fact, he might have been described as a saint.

How did it happen that Manasseh came to repent of his evil ways? In his youth and early manhood he gave himself without restraint to evildoing until the cup of the judgment and wrath of God was full. Captured among the thorns, bound with chains, and imprisoned in faraway Babylon, he had time and occasion to reflect on the error of his ways. One tradition indicates that in prison he was fed a subsistence diet consisting of a mixture of water, vinegar, and bran. (There's a menu that would be inclined to lead a prodigal king to "come to himself"!) Another apocryphal record indicates that Manasseh was placed in an iron horse which was then heated to an almost unbearable temperature. Under these stressful circumstances he came to a realization that the way of the transgressor is hard.

The Scriptures make it clear that Manasseh's repentance was indeed sincere:

> *And when he was in affliction, he besought the Lord his God, and he humbled himself greatly before the God of his fathers, and prayed unto him: and he was entreated of him, and heard his supplication, and brought him again to Jerusalem into his kingdom. Then Manasseh knew that the Lord he was God* (II Chron. 33:12-13).

Yes, Manasseh truly repented. He literally and drastically changed his mind about sin. He saw his sin, all sin, in the light of the holiness and righteousness of God. But his repentance was more than a mere intellectual attitude. It involved his total personality, including his emotions and his will. He was sorry for his sins. They grieved him deeply. His heart was not only broken for his sin, but *from* his sin. He was resolved, with the help of the God of Israel, to be through with his evil ways. And he was determined to do all that he could to undo the sad consequences of his years of unrestrained evil living and his leadership in the direction of pagan practices in his nation.

Upon his return to the throne in Jerusalem, Manasseh took away the strange gods, and "cast . . . out of the city" the idols which he had placed in the sacred temple of Jehovah. In addition, "he repaired the altar of the Lord, and sacrificed thereon peace offerings and thank offerings, and commanded Judah to serve the Lord God of Israel" (II Chron. 33:16).

Manasseh is to be commended for his earnest efforts to undo the personal and collective damage which flowed from his earlier, wicked life. But the effort was largely futile. The consequences were irreparable. To some degree the people followed his exhortations to return to righteous living. But the effort was halfhearted and only modestly successful.

As is so often the case, the evil influence of Manasseh's early life had indelibly marked the character and conduct of his son and successor, Amon. The Word of God is unusually frank and explicit at this point: "Amon was two and twenty years old when he began to reign, and reigned two years in Jerusalem. But he did that which was evil in the sight of the Lord, as did Manasseh his father: for Amon sacrificed unto all the carved images which Manasseh his father had made, and served them; and humbled not himself before the Lord, as Manasseh his father had humbled himself; but Amon trespassed more and more. And his servants conspired against him, and slew him in his own house" (II Chron. 33:21-24).

The kingdom of Judah did not collapse immediately. But the damage had been done. The moral and spiritual foundations had been crumbling slowly away. Total collapse was but a matter of time. And Manasseh, the sinner who became a saint, was largely to blame. And he knew it. His latter years must have been a strange mixture of satisfaction for having turned resolutely from his evil ways and poignant regret as he saw the inevitable consequences of his earlier, wayward life taking their unhappy toll in the life of his own family and nation.

A wise Christian leader once said, "I have had two constructive fears in my life. One was that I might neglect or refuse the call of the Lord Jesus Christ and His gracious offer of mercy and salvation, and lose my soul forever. The other fear was that I, as a Christian, might waste my time and energies in trivial and transient endeavors and, like the unwise Christians of whom the Apostle Paul wrote, build my structure of character and service of materials

94

comparable to wood, hay, and stubble (I Cor. 3:10-15). The result would then be irreparable loss when my service and works were tested by God's fiery judgment of works."

The poignant story of Manasseh suggests another fear which should motivate a thoughtful person. It is this: a wholesome, godly fear of the inevitable physical, social, and moral consequences of sinful living.

The idea that every young person should "have his fling" or should "sow his wild oats" in youth hardly commends itself to thoughtful and observant people. The experience of Manasseh, and millions of others since his day, fails to support the view that even a young person can violate God's moral laws with impunity.

Our sins may be forgiven by grace through faith in the Lord Jesus Christ and the acceptance of the benefits of His vicarious, atoning work on the Cross. We may be gloriously pardoned, freely justified by faith. The power of sin may be broken, and eternal death, the penalty of sin, may be cancelled. Yet we continue to live in a moral universe. It is still basically true that "whatsoever a man soweth, that shall he also reap." The laws of sowing and reaping in the physical, mental, and social realms are relentless and impartial in their operation. They are the laws of a completely dependable God. They reflect His absolute consistency and integrity.

Consequently, while a gracious, forgiving God may freely pardon a guilty sinner for Jesus Christ's sake, the inevitable and often tragic and painful biological, physical, mental, or social consequences of that sin may continue on for a lifetime, or even for generations. In this sense, the sins of the fathers may fall on innocent children of generations yet unborn. Does anyone ever sin with impunity without someone else being hurt in one way or another?

What, then, is the counsel of wisdom? What does the story of Manasseh say to you and me? What guidance for discriminating living can we derive from Manasseh's poignant experience, which a great preacher has aptly called "the hell of a good man"?

The central lesson of Manasseh's experience is well summed up by "the Preacher" in Eccles. 12:1, "Remember now thy Creator in the days of thy youth, while the evil days come not, nor the years draw nigh, when thou shalt say, I have no pleasure in them." And is it not the part of wisdom that each of us should never, never forget the closing admonition of the wise man when he said, "Let us hear the conclusion of the whole matter: Fear God, and keep his commandments: for this is the whole duty of man. For God shall bring every work into judgment, with every secret thing, whether it be good, or whether it be evil" (Eccles. 12:13-14)?

11

ESAU:
The Sacramental Principle of Life

There are two kinds of twins: identical and fraternal. Identical twins develop from the same ovum, and have exactly the same set of genes, the carriers of hereditary traits. As a result, they are always of the same sex, have very similar intelligence quotients, and often look so much alike that it is difficult to tell them apart. In contrast, fraternal twins develop from two separate ova, with different sets of genes. They are no more alike genetically than children of the same parents born years apart. They may or may not be of the same sex.

Esau was one of the most famous twins mentioned in the Bible. The evidence is conclusive that he and his brother, Jacob, were not identical twins. The story of their lives tends to emphasize their differences in appearance,

temperament, interests, loyalties, and spiritual responsiveness. The persistent struggle between them and their
descendants began, in fact, before the twins were born.
And it continues to this day in the Jewish-Arab rivalry of
the Middle East.

The family situation into which these twins were born
was far from ideal. Rebekah, their mother, was a decisive,
vigorous, domineering, possessive, daring, and adventurous person. At times she was somewhat unscrupulous in
her efforts to gain her objectives, which usually involved
the interests of her favorite son, Jacob.

Isaac, the father of the boys, was a quiet, meek,
retiring, easygoing type of man. He had probably been
overdependent on his mother, Sarah, who was an exceptionally strong personality. His pattern of overdependency
tended to continue in his relationship to his wife, Rebekah.

Jacob, Esau's brother, is described in the Scriptures
as a "smooth" man. He was crafty, shrewd, calculating.
His very name meant "heel-grasper" or "supplanter." Despite his deceptive and devious tendencies, he was a man
of spiritual responsiveness with respect for the religious
and spiritual heritage of the family.

Esau, the oldest of the twins, was a red, hairy man—a
hunter who loved the outdoors. Temperamentally, he was
impulsive, even to the point of occasional rashness. Earthbound, sensuous Esau was largely devoid of respect for
the spiritual tradition of the family. He was his father's
favorite—for the revealing and dubious reason that Isaac
"did eat of his venison."

The courtship and marriage of Isaac and Rebekah is
one of the most beautiful, romantic love stories recorded
in the Bible. But the marriage and family relationship de-
teriorated as the twins came into the home and favoritism
toward the children developed. Deception and intrigue
followed. What had begun as a beautiful love-match dis-

integrated into sordid, scheming, conniving situations permeated by ill will, hatred, suspicion, and vulgarity.

Despite certain character defects, there is much to
admire in Esau. He was a cunning and brave hunter, a man
of the wide-open spaces. Though impulsive, he could be
warm and friendly, as well as dark and dangerous. He was
not a sullen, vindictive person. It was apparently difficult
for him to carry a grudge for long. In contrast to his scheming brother, he was usually open and generous in his attitudes.

What, then, was the crucial defect in Esau's character?
Why is he alone identified in the Scriptures as a *profane*
man? The answer seems to be that he combined his mother's insensitivity to spiritual values with an impulsive,
ungovernable, undisciplined, animal-like nature. The result was that he was sensuous, earthbound. He lacked an
awareness of and responsiveness to spiritual values. He
counted them as something common, of little or no worth.
He did not recognize or respond to the claims of Almighty
God upon his life. In this respect he was a profane man.

Esau's profanity is revealed in two principal incidents
in his life: the sale of his birthright to Jacob, and his marriage to Hittite women.

The first incident may have occurred when Esau was
a teen-ager. Coming in from the hunt, weary and raven-
ously hungry, he found his brother preparing a savory
meal. Immediately the bargaining began. Esau's request,
so typical of him, was, "Let me swallow [gulp down] some
of this red stuff, for I am faint." Jacob, the schemer, was
quick with his shrewd proposition, "Sell me first thy birthright . . . swear to me." So, the record tells us, "he sware
unto him: and he sold his birthright unto Jacob. . . . and
he did eat and drink . . . and went his way" (Gen. 25:
33-34). Thus it was that Esau, the earthbound Edomite,
"despised his birthright."

It was a foolish and serious act to sell his birthright,

for this constituted an insult to Jehovah. The birthright carried not only a claim to a double portion of Isaac's possessions and certain rights of family leadership, but it also conveyed the right of priesthood and the privilege of bestowing special spiritual blessings and privileges on the children of the family.

Esau did not display aggressive insult toward this precious, valuable, and sacred birthright. No, he merely *despised* it. He counted it of little worth. That which was inherently sacred was looked upon as common and cheap. He was guilty of the sin of profanity—treating as secular and common that which was holy and sacred.

The second incident which reveals Esau's lack of sensitivity toward spiritual values occurred when he was a full-grown man, 40 years of age. Against the wishes of both of his parents, and doubtless also the known will of God, he deliberately married two idolatrous, sensual Hittite women. This was probably a deliberate, calculated, vindictive act, the consequence of years of association with the pagan Hittites.

From Esau's unholy marriages there sprang a group of people, the Edomites, known for their ruthless, irreligious character. The three Herods of the New Testament, infamous for their heartless cruelty and unrestrained sensuality, were notable descendants of Esau.

The sin of profanity is far more inclusive than merely taking the sacred name of God in vain. It is treating anything that is holy or sacred as common or cheap. In our day, the sin of profanity is often identified with secularism. The latter has been well defined as the organization of life as if God did not exist; or if He does exist, as if it doesn't matter much. Secularism is thus a kind of practical, lived-out atheism. It is without question a major enemy of the Church of Jesus Christ in contemporary American culture.

What is the New Testament answer to the sin of profanity or secularism? It is *holiness as hallowedness!* Or, to put it another way, it is the *maintenance of a sacramental view of the whole of life.*

In the words of the Apostle Paul, God's rejoinder to the profanation of life is found in these challenging words: "Whether therefore ye eat, or drink, or whatsoever ye do, do all to the glory of God" (I Cor. 10:31).

This simply means that, for the New Testament follower of the Lord Jesus Christ, the whole of life is sacred. Each and every aspect of life is to be kept in a dynamic relationship to the will of God. This is holiness in action. When this is achieved, life is destined to reach its highest degree of hallowedness and fulfillment. Every facet of life is sanctified and glows with divine sacredness and radiance.

Let us consider for a moment the nature of a true sacrament. Protestants, for the most part, accept only two sacraments as valid: the Lord's Supper and water baptism. In every true sacrament there is a *physical* sign and a *spiritual* seal. In the Lord's Supper, the bread and wine (physical) signify the spiritual reality of the atoning sacrifice of our Lord Jesus Christ. In baptism, the water represents the regenerating work of the Holy Spirit. A true sacrament, then, *always* involves a physical element and a spiritual meaning. Only as these two are kept in a dynamic and faithful relationship to one another, each the expression of the other, does a true sacramental relationship exist.

In its broadest application the sacramental principle represents the divine plan for the ideal relationship between the entire material and spiritual realms. G. A. Studdert-Kennedy describes this relationship in an excerpt of religious verse entitled, "Set Your Affections on Things Above":

> *How far above the things of earth*
> *Is Christ at God's right hand?*

How far above yon snowy peaks
  Do His white angels stand?
Must we fare forth to seek a world
  Beyond that silent star?
Forsake these dear familiar homes
  And climb the heights? How far?

As far as meaning is from speech,
  As beauty from a rose,
As far as music is from sound,
  As poetry from prose,

As far as art from cleverness,
  As painting is from paints,
As far as sign from sacraments,
  As Pharisees from saints,

As far as love from friendship is,
  As reason is from truth,
As far as laughter is from joy,
  And early years from youth,

As far as love from shining eyes,
  As passion from a kiss,
So far is God from God's green earth,
  So far that world from this. *

God's answer to the profanation and secularization of life is this sacramental view of the whole of life. It is Christian consecration in action and application, every day in the week and in every area of the common life. What does this conception mean in the area of practical living? Very much indeed. Time and space permit only three specific illustrations.

First, the body of each born-again Christian is to be thought of as a sacred temple. Listen again to the Apostle

---

*G. A. Studdert-Kennedy, *The Unutterable Beauty* (London: Hodder and Stoughton, Ltd., 1927), p. 151. Used by permission.

102

Paul: "What? know ye not that your body is the temple of the Holy Ghost . . . ? therefore glorify God in your body . . . which . . . [is] God's" (I Cor. 6:19-20). The body and its functions are sacred—a holy temple devoted to God.

The Temple of ancient Israel was dedicated to God, as a whole, and each and every part in particular. This was done in a purposeful manner with a special prayer of dedication. The Temple was accepted by God, indwelt by His holy presence, and became the means by which He manifested himself to men.

In like manner, the body of each follower of the Lord Jesus Christ, as a whole and in each particular part, is to be presented to Him as a living sacrifice (Rom. 12:1-2). This is to be done as an act of intelligent worship, in response to the acknowledged mercies of God, in a special, purposeful act of dedication. The Christian's yielded body is then indwelt by the Holy Spirit of God as a sacred temple, and becomes the medium by which He is made known to others.

The profanation of the body and its functions concerns many thoughtful observers of contemporary American culture. Violence and sadistic brutality are glorified with disgusting unconcern. Sex is flaunted before millions, including children of all ages, as an end in itself. All of these tendencies, together with morbid over-concern with the body and its functions, or carelessness with reference to proper care, violate the basic principle of the essential hallowedness of the body as the holy temple of the Spirit of God.

When God is glorified in and through the body, a person will neither neglect nor despise its functions. They will be viewed as basically good, when used to attain God-ordained objectives and fulfill divinely approved purposes. There will be an intelligent, balanced discipline of the body and its functions. Tendencies to elevate the sensual above the mental and spiritual will be assiduously avoided and rejected. Recreation will be interpreted in truly Christian terms and as genuinely re-creating. Approval will be given only to those activities which leave a person stronger physically, clearer mentally, and unsullied spiritually.

The principle of the sacredness of the whole of life, including the body and its functions, has special relevance in the area of sex. The problems here will be viewed in terms of the total context of the high and holy purpose God had in creating the two sexes, and instituting permanent, monogamous marriage as the ideal. The physical aspects of sex will never be divorced from the spiritual as reflected in genuine love at its finest and best, and which can be truly and fully expressed only in the marriage relationship. Sex functions will never be divorced from persons, for this tends to violate the sacramental principle and reduces a person to the status of a thing to be used. And this is *never* right. God's plan is always that we shall *use things*, and *love persons*—never the reverse.

The principle of the sacramental relationship of sex and genuine love is one of the most elevating and guiding principles for any couple, either before or after marriage. When and to the degree that the sacramental ideal is attained, life is fulfilled and filled full of happiness and joy. And whenever and to the degree that the ideal is not attained, life is unfulfilled and tends to deteriorate.

St. Paul was right, and experience validates the principle: "Whether therefore ye eat, or drink, or whatsoever ye do, do all to the glory of God." The result is always and universally the same when the ideal is approximated: life becomes hallowed with a divine radiance and significance!

A second illustration of the principle of the sacramental view of the whole of life is that the work of every Spirit-filled Christian becomes a *vocation*—a calling of God. Note these words of the Apostle Paul as he speaks to the Christians in the church at Corinth: "Let every man abide in the same calling wherein he was called. Ye are bought with

104

a price; be not ye the servants of men. Brethren, let every man, wherein he is called, therein abide with God" (I Cor. 7:20, 23-24).

The New Testament standard, "Whatsoever ye do, do all to the glory of God," assuredly applies to every Christian's lifework. St. Paul declares that we are not to be servants of men, but of God, who is to be brought into our work as an active Partner.

In the Early Church, the work of Christian laymen such as Aquila and Priscilla, co-workers with Paul, was viewed as a ministry. The word *vocation* means a "calling," and becomes meaningless unless Someone calls. Work to which God calls a Christian thus becomes a means of loving, serving, and honoring God and building His kingdom among men.

During the Middle Ages three levels of service developed. These included, first, the life of contemplation, the monastic, which was looked upon as the highest. A second level was that of the secular priest, who lived according to the "rule" but in contact with human affairs. The lowest level was that of the common workman or layman. Martin Luther reacted violently against these distinctions, which he felt were not supported by the New Testament. He asserted the doctrine of the priesthood of all believers, and held that the work of the lowliest peasant or the humblest housemaid was sacramental if performed for the glory of God.

If a born-again Christian's vocation is viewed as a sacred calling of God, what does this imply? It means that he will sincerely seek God's will in the choice of a vocation in the first place. He knows that some types of work, destructive of life's highest values, are simply not open to him as a follower of Jesus Christ. Such a Christian will also avoid work that is trivial. He will choose work that is somehow vital and meaningful to mankind. A sacramental view of vocation suggests that a primary concern of such

105

a Christian will be the highest interests of the *people* with whom he works. He will make the quality of his work, his loyalty to his employer, and his dependability a means of witnessing for his Lord. Prayer and meditation will be utilized as a means for creatively serving his Master, his Copartner, in his vocation. He will truly abide in his calling with God.

A third illustration and practical application of the principle of the hallowedness of all of life is that marriage will be viewed as a sacred relationship. The secularization of marriage concerns many who view with increasing concern the problem of divorce and broken homes in our culture. But as we see marriage more and more clearly in terms of the purposes and plan of God, we see it as essentially a sacred relationship.

The marriage relationship is used by the Apostle Paul as one of the three great analogies depicting the intimate, loving, spiritual, mystical relationship between the Lord Jesus Christ and His bride, the Church. As the apostle closes his wonderful discourse on this subject in Ephesians, chapter 5, he seems almost overwhelmed by the mystery of the sacred relationship and exclaims, "This is a great mystery." Years later, St. Jerome, in translating this phrase into the common Latin, put it this way: "This is a great sacrament." On the basis of this translation, marriage became one of the seven sacraments of the Roman Catholic church, by means of which grace is presumed to be channeled from God through the Church to man.

At the time of the Protestant Reformation, marriage as a sacrament was rejected by Protestants, who held that all sacraments must have been clearly instituted by Christ and practiced in the Primitive Church. Therefore, while Protestants denied marriage as a sacrament in the narrow Roman Catholic sense, the relationship was viewed as far more than a mere legal, physical, or psychological union. As we view marriage in terms of the total, divine context,

106

we see it as a permanent, sacred relationship, to be entered into only after careful consideration and prayer in the fear of God, and performed by a Christian minister in the fellowship of believers. In a broad sense, then, marriage as a sacred, permanent relationship is indeed a means of grace, saving individuals from many temptations to sin, and bringing husband and wife to personal fulfillment in the plan of God for their own lives and their children. What a revolution would result in many American homes if this sacramental ideal should be brought in as an active principle in the relationship of husband and wife!

The writer of the Epistle to the Hebrews warns us to diligently watch "lest any man fail of the grace of God; lest any root of bitterness springing up trouble you, and thereby many be defiled; lest there be any fornicator, or profane person, as Esau, who for one morsel of meat sold his birthright" (Heb. 12:15-16). In order to avoid the sin of being profane persons, the writer urges us to "follow peace with all men, and holiness, without which no man shall see the Lord" (Heb. 12:14).

The sacramental view of the whole of life, living all of life for the glory of God—this is God's rejoinder to the sin of secularism or profanity. In God's plan there is no such thing as a religious *department* of life. Whatever cannot be sacramentally related to His will is a problem to be solved or an evil to be destroyed. The whole of life is to be sacred; the body a holy temple, our work a divine vocation, and marriage a symbol of the relationship between Christ and His bride, the Church. "Whether therefore ye eat, or drink, or whatsoever ye do, do all to the glory of God" (I Cor. 10:31).

12

AHITHOPHEL:
Finding Hope for the Hopeless

Suicide is one of the serious personal and social problems of our time. The World Health Organization estimates that 1,000 persons commit suicide each day, and 8,000 attempt to do so and fail. In the United States the annual rate of suicide is 11 per 100,000 persons. This amounts to an average of one person every 24 minutes, or a total of approximately 22,000 such tragedies each year.

In 1920 self-destruction was twenty-second among the causes of death in the United States. Since then there has been a marked increase. Today it is the tenth most common cause of death in our society as a whole, fourth among teen-agers, and second among college students.

There are 11 countries in the Western world where the

suicide rate exceeds that of the United States. Unusually high rates are found in Switzerland, Austria, and Denmark; and low rates in Norway, Holland, Ireland, and Spain.

Three times as many men commit suicide as women, but three times as many women threaten to do so and don't, or attempt to do so and fail. The probability of suicide is greater if a person is white, divorced, mentally ill, age 45 or older, from a broken home, or has a parent who is an alcoholic. A study of 50 children who attempted suicide indicated that virtually all of them looked upon the action as a "last resort." In many cases, there was a history of a near relative having attempted suicide. In one out of four such cases, that relative was a parent.

A surprising number of persons commit suicide by accident. They only intend to threaten or manipulate other people. They "fake" a suicide but carry things too far, and die without really planning to do so. Their suicide notes seldom reveal the true reasons for their actions. One distinguished scholar who studied 3,064 cases of self-destruction over a period of 10 years in the city of Chicago concluded that four out of five (80 percent) of these persons really wanted someone to stop them from carrying out their desperate acts.

Every suicidal act is tragic, but it is especially so when the person has an outstanding reputation for nobility of character, or acknowledged potential for productive living and service. This was the case in the tragedy of Ahithophel, grandfather of Bath-sheba.

The Jews and early Christians had a very high regard for the sacredness and value of life. Consequently, there are only a few cases of self-destruction recorded in the Bible. Most of these occurred under great duress. In one instance, Abimelech, son of Gideon, commanded his armor-bearer to slay him after he had been mortally wounded in battle by a millstone dropped from a tower by a woman. He was greatly concerned lest it should be reported that he had been slain by a woman. In the situation involving King Saul and his armor-bearer, the battle situation appeared hopeless, and suicide was chosen as an alternative to being tortured and slain by the Philistines. The suicides of Samson and Judas Iscariot came as climaxes to complex sequences of tragic and stressful events. The same was true for Ahithophel, yet his act of self-destruction was more calculated and deliberate than any of the others. What chain of unfortunate events led him to this moment of calm desperation?

In the days of King David, and his handsome, long-haired son, Absalom, the name Ahithophel was virtually synonymous with the "wisdom of God." The Word of God declares that "the counsel of Ahithophel, which he counselled in those days, was as if a man had inquired at the oracle of God: so was all the counsel of Ahithophel both with David and with Absalom" (II Sam. 16:23).

For years David and Ahithophel were very close associates. David respected, feared, and followed the advice of the older and wiser man. Ahithophel's son, Eliam, was a member of David's personal bodyguard, and was one of his 37 "mighty men" of war. The beautiful daughter of Eliam, Bath-sheba, was Ahithophel's granddaughter. She was the wife of another of David's leading warriors, Uriah the Hittite.

Bath-sheba was doubtless the pride and joy of her grandfather. She had been recently and happily married to Uriah. Although he was not an Israelite, Uriah was not only a brave and able warrior, but a man whose loyalty and devotion to King David were beyond question.

The unusual qualities of Uriah were revealed in his behavior when he was called from the battlefield by David, who was anxious to cover up his adulterous relationship with Bath-sheba (II Samuel 11). When Uriah refused, because of loyalty to the cause of Judah and his fellow soldiers, to follow David's suggestions, David ordered what, in effect, was Uriah's execution. Joab, David's commander in chief, was ordered to place Uriah in a vulnerable position in the front ranks of the troops. The anticipated result was achieved. Uriah was slain (II Sam. 11:14-27).

After Uriah's murder, David married the pregnant Bath-sheba. This marriage was followed by the indictment of David's adulterous and murderous conduct by Nathan, God's courageous prophet. Despite David's sincere repentance and earnest prayer, the child who had been conceived in this illicit affair died.

Can you imagine what a knowledge of these immoral and tragic events did to the aged Ahithophel? The violation of his beautiful granddaughter, the callous murder of her valorous and faithful husband—these events must have crushed the dreams and hopes of the old man. To think that the king, to whom he had been as the oracle of God, could do these vile things must have wounded his sensitive spirit beyond compare, and shaken his confidence in the poet-king beyond repair.

With these tragic events as a backdrop, the winsome and astute son of David, Absalom, entered the picture. He shrewdly laid plans to win the loyalty of his father's followers, and take over the throne by force. Absalom was undoubtedly well acquainted with all the events surrounding the relationship of David, Bath-sheba, Eliam, Uriah, and Ahithophel. Consequently when he thought that the time was ripe for his *coup d'etat*, "Absalom sent for Ahithophel the Gilonite, David's counsellor, from his city, even from Giloh, while he offered sacrifices" (II Sam. 15:12). And Ahithophel came and joined in the revolt against David.

The high regard that David had for Ahithophel and the latter's counsel is reflected in the king's response when he heard this news. David prayed earnestly that the Lord would turn the "counsel of Ahithophel into foolishness" (II Sam. 15:31).

But David did more than pray! He sent an astute and

loyal friend, Hushai, as a spy into the camp of Absalom. Hushai's assignment was to counter and thwart the advice of Ahithophel. And David's strategy succeeded.

Ahithophel's relationship to Absalom was marked by two crucial acts. The old man first advised the attractive young prince to publicly violate the integrity of his father's harem by shamelessly and publicly going in unto the 10 concubines whom David had left in Jerusalem (II Sam. 16: 20-23). This act fulfilled a dire prophecy made by the prophet Nathan concerning David's violation of Bathsheba:

> Thus saith the Lord, Behold, I will raise up evil against thee out of thine own house, and I will take thy wives before thine eyes, and give them unto thy neighbour, and he shall lie with thy wives in the sight of this sun. For thou didst it secretly: but I will do this thing before all Israel, and before the sun (II Sam. 12:11-12).

By this act, the "die was cast" for both Absalom and Ahithophel! Now there was no turning back. The revolt must succeed—or else! Both men had now "crossed their Rubicons."

What should be done now? Ahithophel urged Absalom to strike decisively and immediately against David's disorganized forces. While this advice pleased Absalom somewhat, he also asked the advice of Hushai, David's loyal friend. Hushai urged Absalom not to follow Ahithophel's counsel, but to delay any action until the battle might be joined in a more formal fashion (II Sam. 17:6-14).

Absalom and his associates chose to accept the advice of Hushai and reject that of Ahithophel. And Hushai, as a good spy, proceeded at once to inform David of the decision (II Sam. 17:15-22).

The sequel to all of this is recorded in these poignant words: "And when Ahithophel saw that his counsel was not followed, he saddled his ass, and arose, and gat him home to his house, to his city, and put his household in order, and hanged himself, and died, and was buried in the sepulchre of his father" (II Sam. 17:23). Is there a sadder verse in all of the Old Testament than this one?

The revolt of Absalom was soon to end. As he was caught by his heavy hair in the branches of an oak tree, his heart was pierced by three darts in the cruel hands of ruthless Joab, David's military commander, who had carried out David's callous and cynical order concerning Uriah's murder.

The stark tragedy of all these interwoven events is echoed in the heartbroken wail of King David when he heard of his gifted son's death, "O my son Absalom, my son, my son Absalom! would God I had died for thee, O Absalom, my son, my son!" (II Sam. 18:33) But one wonders how many sad memories are also included of the wise and kindly Ahithophel, the brave and loyal Eliam and Uriah, and the pliable and voluptuous Bath-sheba.

David's despairing cry was not for Absalom alone. It was for himself. It is reminiscent of the oft repeated truism, "Though the mills of God grind slowly, yet they grind exceeding small."

Why did a wise man, a good man, a kindly man deliberately call his family together, set his house in order, put a rope around his neck, and end his life? The answer: His situation, as he perceived it, was *absolutely hopeless.* It was an act of last resort. He could see no other way out.

This despairing hopelessness is the "final, common motive" which leads people to terminate their earthly lives prematurely.

A small proportion of those who destroy themselves are mentally ill. They may suffer from hallucinations or delusions. They sometimes become fixated on or obsessed with the idea of death. Others may suffer from "temporary insanity" and commit suicide impulsively as a result of some overwhelming problem such as a financial reverse or disappointment in love. Occasionally a person will develop a

113

long-term masochistic pattern of self-mutilation or destruction. Some destroy themselves bit by bit through the use of drugs or the excessive use of alcohol.

Psychiatrists have usually centered their attention on the various personal reasons for self-destruction. The list of such motives is long: an intolerable loss of self-respect or self-esteem, an unbearable feeling of loneliness, a crushing sense of inferiority and inadequacy, an overwhelming sense of meaninglessness, a desire to escape from intense competition, the loss of loved ones, a senile loss of the "will to live," and so on.

Sociologists have concentrated their attention on the social order and its bearing on suicide. A widely held view is that social disorganization is directly related to the rate of suicide. If there is a large amount of group solidarity and mutual support, the suicide rate is low. Of course, the general attitude of a society toward suicide is an important factor. In certain societies, suicide may not only be allowed but it may become the "honorable" thing to do.

In his recent book, *Theory of Suicide*, M. L. Farber has endeavored to integrate the personal and social factors in suicide. He concludes that the common core factor is "despairing hopelessness." This is the common denominator of the problem from both the personal and the social viewpoints. How can an individual whose situation is desperate acquire new hope? How can the community—the social order, the church, the family—provide the sustaining hope which the person in deep trouble needs?

One thing is crystal-clear: The Word of God contains a message of vibrant and sustaining hope. In the Old Testament there is a repeated refrain: The only sure hope of Israel is in God (Ps. 78:7; Jer. 14:7-8; etc.). The prophet Joel declared that "the Lord will be the hope [place of repair or harbor] of his people, and the strength of the children of Israel" (3:16). Though Jeremiah lived in chaotic and troubled times with overwhelming political and social

114

disorganization, he still insisted, "Blessed is the man that trusteth in the Lord, and whose hope the Lord is" (17:7).

In the New Testament the gospel, the Good News of salvation through the Lord Jesus Christ, is charged with exhilarating hope. The Apostle Paul declared, "Whatsoever things were written aforetime were written for our learning, that we through patience and comfort of the scriptures might have hope" (Rom. 15:4). And the apostle added this prayer, "Now the God of hope fill you with all joy and peace in believing, that ye may abound in hope, through the power of the Holy Ghost" (Rom. 15:13). Paul further declared that "we are saved by hope" (Rom. 8:24); and that Jesus Christ himself indwells each believer as the "hope of glory" (Col. 1:27). The second return of the Lord Jesus Christ is referred to as "that blessed hope" (Titus 2:13); and the writer to the Hebrews gave this strong word of assurance: "That . . . we might have a strong consolation, who have fled for refuge to lay hold upon the hope set before us: which hope we have as an anchor of the soul, both sure and stedfast, and which entereth into that within the veil" (Heb. 6:18-19).

Concerning the hope of the Christians, the Apostle Peter declared, "Blessed be the God and Father of our Lord Jesus Christ, which according to his abundant mercy hath begotten us again unto a lively hope by the resurrection of Jesus Christ from the dead" (I Pet. 1:3). Yes, a genuine, born-again Christian is a person with a *lively hope*. It is dynamic, thrilling, strength-imparting. And a Spirit-filled, Spirit-led Christian community is one which is permeated by this living, sustaining hope.

Dr. Farber, in his penetrating study of the personal and social factors in suicide, declares, "Suicide will be reduced by the introduction into society of sources of hope, of institutions that foster the sense of competence, that supply something of succorance and even love."

What a challenge this poses for you and me as individual followers of the Lord Jesus Christ, and for the Christian communities of which we are a part! Do we as individuals—do our Christian communities—generate enough dynamic, lively hope to provide an anti-suicidal force for those around us who may be on the verge of despair? Do our personal lives and testimonies and our fellowship experiences convince others that our God is indeed the God of hope? Are they likely to be convinced that the Christian faith provides a triumphant hope in the face of even death itself?

The Christian cannot condone suicide as a "way out." And yet he must show love and sympathy toward all those whose lives are touched and wounded by these tragedies. More people around us than we realize may be on the verge of despair. Our culture is marked by social mobility, urbanization, with its increasing depersonalization, and intense economic and social competition. All these may combine to drive many people to the point of despair. And who knows? Someone whose heart is almost breaking may be living in your block, residing in the next apartment, or even sitting beside you in church.

13

ELIAKIM:
Invisible Means of Support

W. H. Auden describes the twentieth century as "the age of anxiety." As a result of the pressures of life, many people reach the end of their resources. Psychiatrist William Menninger estimates that at least 10 percent of the population of the United States need psychiatric help. On the average, one out of 16 persons will spend some time in a mental hospital before he dies. A million citizens are mentally ill; 8 million are neurotic; another million or more are alcoholics; and 100,000 attempt suicide each year. One out of eight draftees in World War II was rejected because of personality problems, and the most common cause for separation from the armed forces was labelled "psychoneurotic casualty." The anxieties and tensions of life overwhelm many people. Their capacity to tolerate frustration, conflict, and anxiety is too low.

Eliakim, the man whose life story is presented here,

also lived in an era of great conflict, fear, and tension. He had the capacity to meet the crises of his day without breaking down under pressure. Morally, spiritually, and psychologically he proved that "he could take it." He had adequate frustration tolerance. This is that aspect of personality and character which enables a person to withstand psychological or moral stress successfully. It is the ability to "take" whatever pressures life may bring without "cracking up" or "breaking down" emotionally, mentally, or morally. Without doubt, it is one of the ingredients of a healthy Christian personality. It is an essential element in that resilient strength which marks a person as both secure and mature psychologically.

Eliakim, whose name meant, "My God, He shall arise," was empowered and used by Almighty God in a great crisis in the history of Judah. This obscure man became a savior to his nation, an honor to his father's house, and a type of our Lord Jesus Christ. Let us look at the historical setting which brought him into the spotlight on the stage of history. It was a time that tried men's souls.

Hezekiah, one of the more devout kings of Judah, was in the fourth year of his reign when the panzer divisions of Shalmaneser, king of Assyria, laid siege to Samaria, capital of the Northern Kingdom (Israel). After three years the city was taken and the inhabitants were carried away into captivity. Ten years later Sennacherib, who now directed the Assyrian blitzkrieg, came up against the fortified cities of Judah (the Southern Kingdom) and took them. In dismay, Hezekiah offered to pay a huge ransom to the Assyrians, even to the extent of stripping the gold and silver from the temple of God. But the arrogant, blustering Assyrian despot sent his envoys to the very gates of Jerusalem. There, in insolent, haughty language they insulted Judah's king and people, and blasphemed the true and living God of Israel.

In desperation, Hezekiah sent his trusted household

steward, or treasurer, Eliakim, to the prophet Isaiah for advice. After consulting the Lord, the prophet gave a reassuring reply concerning the proud and ruthless Sennacherib:

"But I know your sitting down and your going out and coming in, and your raging against me. Because you have raged against me and your arrogance has come into my ears, I will put my hook in your nose and my bit in your mouth, and I will turn you back on the way by which you came" (II Kings 19:27-28, RSV).

And that very night the angel of the Lord slew 185,000 Assyrian soldiers. In dismay, Sennacherib returned to his capital, Nineveh. Shortly afterward, he was murdered by two of his sons as he worshipped in the house of his heathen god, Nisroch (II Kings 19:37).

But this wasn't all that happened in this devastating crisis in Judah's history. At the outset, a Gentile, Shebna, was the king's steward or treasurer. This was a position of high trust and great responsibility. Under the pressure of the crisis, Shebna's personal ambition and pride overcame his sense of integrity and loyalty. He used his position and power for personal, selfish advantage (Isa. 22:15-16). God was greatly displeased, and aroused to stern action. The word of the Lord was:

"Behold, the Lord will hurl you away violently, O you strong man. He will seize firm hold on you, and whirl you round and round, and throw you like a ball into a wide land; there you shall die, and there shall be your splendid chariots, you shame of your master's house. I will thrust you from your office, and you will be cast down from your station" (Isa. 22:17-19, RSV).

Then follows a thrilling statement concerning Eliakim:

"In that day," said the Lord, "I will call my servant Eliakim, the son of Hilkiah, and I will clothe him with your [Shebna's] robe, and will bind your girdle on him, and will commit your authority to his hand; and he shall be a father to the inhabitants of Jerusalem and to the

> house of Judah. And I will place on his shoulder the key
> of the house of David; he shall open, and none shall
> shut; and he shall shut, and none shall open. And I will
> fasten him like a peg in a sure place, and he shall become
> a throne of honor to his father's house" (vv. 20-23, RSV).

So Eliakim became a savior to his nation and an honor
to his father's house. But even more significant, he became
a type of our Lord Jesus Christ. In the message of the risen,
glorified Christ to the Church at Philadelphia, the "Church
of the Open Door," Christ refers to himself in language
first used of Eliakim, "These things saith he that is holy, he
that is true, he that hath the key of David, he that openeth,
and no man shutteth; and shutteth, and no man openeth"
(Rev. 3:7).

Why did Eliakim remain true to his trust under great
pressure? Why did Shebna fail? How can we account for
the moral and psychological frustration tolerance of the
man whom God described as a "nail in a sure place"? One
man failed under stress. The other did not. Why the difference?

Eliakim's ability to stand firm in a time of stress arose
from three sources: the resilient strength of his personality
(character structure), his personal devotion to his nation's
welfare, and the sovereign, providential support of Almighty God.

The Jewish program of character education under
which Eliakim had grown to manhood was designed to provide him with a strong moral character. He had been trained
in realistic, courageous habits of thinking and acting. Jewish
education was closely tied to daily living, line upon line,
precept upon precept. Eliakim's personality structure and
moral character were the product of years of daily living,
and innumerable right and responsible decisions on the
moral battlefields of life.

The result was that when he came to his "big moment"
—when his king and his nation called for his leadership in

a time of crisis—Eliakim was ready. He had acquired a character structure, a life-style, consisting of a group of wholesome, realistic habits of facing life's problems.

He had first made his habits. Now they made him. He had built good habits, and was almost certain to succeed. The older he was, the more like himself he became. He had great flexible strength—like highly tensile steel.

Over the years Eliakim had learned to meet the daily temptations, problems, and tasks of life with realism, fortitude, faith, and tenacity of purpose. Now his moment of destiny had come. Shebna had proven untrue to the trust that his nation had placed in him. Eliakim was called upon to take up the task of leadership. His hour of great trial was but an opportunity to reveal the resilient moral and personality strength he had been building day by day through the years.

A second reason for Eliakim's moral and spiritual strength in the face of apparent disaster is what modern students of personality have called *ego-involvement*. This simply means that his heart was in it. His self-esteem was deeply involved in Judah's success or failure. If worse came to worst, and Jerusalem fell to the invading Assyrians, it would occur only after Eliakim had given the last full measure of his devotion.

Somehow, over the years Eliakim had come to love Judah and its people and ideals. He loved Judah's king, Hezekiah; its prophet, Isaiah; and the God who had chosen Judah as the instrument of His providential purposes.

On several occasions the Scriptures refer to Eliakim as the "son of Hilkiah." We do not know with certainty who Hilkiah was but there is good reason to believe that he was a loyal, faithful, God-fearing son of Abraham. From him Eliakim had caught a spirit of genuine devotion and great fidelity to his nation and its covenant-keeping God.

There is reason to believe, too, that Shebna, who failed

in his loyalty and personal integrity under pressure, was not a "son of Abraham." He was probably an "outsider" who was somehow able to obtain a position of honor and trust in the government of Judah. But he used his position, and the chaos of the times, to promote his own self-interests. His loyalty to Judah was superficial and short-lived.

Shebna did not identify deeply and loyally with the destiny of God's chosen people. In contrast, Eliakim's "heart" was in the effort to save Judah. He was totally committed to winning at all costs. It was "victory or else." The defeat of God's people meant personal defeat for him. The highest values and virtues of his nation had become an integral part of his own character. And the result: He became an honor to his father's house, and a national hero in an hour of destiny.

The third reason for Eliakim's strength and loyalty in Judah's crisis was by all odds the most important. The Word of God makes it crystal-clear that there was one overriding, compelling reason for Eliakim's adequacy in this crucial hour! *Almighty God was supplying invisible means of support!* Notice what the Lord God himself declared: "I will call my servant"; "I will clothe him"; "I will commit your authority to his hand"; "I will place on his shoulder the key of the house of David"; "I will fasten him like a peg in a sure place" (Isa. 22:20-23, RSV).

How could such a man fail with such divine means of support? The answer: *He could not and did not fail!* The sovereign God raised him from obscurity, clothed him with power and authority, opened and closed doors for him, and fastened him "as a nail in a sure place." Little wonder, then, that Eliakim became "a father to the inhabitants of Jerusalem, and to the house of Judah." Almighty God was his sure support, and the ultimate Source of his strength!

In one of the most eloquent and reassuring passages of the New Testament, the Apostle Paul outlines the invisible means of support possessed by every genuine believer in the Lord Jesus Christ.

> *What shall we then say to these things? If God be for us, who can be against us? He that spared not his own Son, but delivered him up for us all, how shall he not with him also freely give us all things? Nay, in all these things we are more than conquerors through him that loved us. For I am persuaded, that neither death, nor life, nor angels, nor principalities, nor powers, nor things present, nor things to come, nor height, nor depth, nor any other creature, shall be able to separate us from the love of God, which is in Christ Jesus our Lord* (Rom. 8:31-32, 37-39).

Comparable assurances of strength, recognition, and companionship are given by the risen, glorified Christ, of whom Eliakim is a type, to His disciples who are confronted with the "great tribulation." Here are His reassuring words:

> *"I have set before thee an open door, and no man can shut it . . . I also will keep thee from the hour of temptation, which shall come upon all the world, to try them that dwell upon the earth. Him that overcometh will I make a pillar in the temple of my God, and he shall go no more out: and I will write upon him the name of . . . the city of my God, which is new Jerusalem, which cometh down out of heaven from my God: and I will write upon him my new name"* (Rev. 3:8, 10, 12).

Eliakim, an ordinary, unknown man, identified his insignificant life with the great, triumphant, ongoing purposes of Almighty God. The inevitable result: He remained loyal and true in the midst of a momentous personal and national crisis. As a consequence he became, under God, a blessing to his people, an honor to his father's house, a source of inspiration to you and me, and a type of our Lord Jesus Christ.

Eliakim had learned that God's tide is sure to win. And we should never forget that all the divine resources which were available to Eliakim, and more, are available to those who, through Christ, link their little lives to the ongoing purposes of the Eternal God.

WAVE AND TIDE

On the far reef the breakers
   Recoil in shattered foam.
Yet still the sea behind them
   Urges its forces home.
Its chant of triumph surges
   Through all the thunderous din;
The wave may break in failure,
   But the tide is sure to win!

The reef is strong and cruel;
   Upon its jagged wall
One wave—a score—a hundred,
   Broken and beaten, fall.
Yet in defeat they conquer.
   The sea comes flooding in;
Wave upon wave is routed,
   But the tide is sure to win.

O mighty sea! Thy message
   In clanging spray is cast;
Within God's plan of progress
   It matters not at last
How wide the shores of evil,
   How strong the reefs of sin—
The wave may be defeated,
   But the tide is sure to win.

        —Priscilla Leonard
        Outlook, 1911

14

DANIEL:
Reaching Life's Fullest Measure

Daniel is one of the best known and most admired men of the Bible. He lived vitally, richly, fully, and usefully. He was what some modern students of personality would call a "fully self-actualized person." With the help of God, he was able to live up to and develop much of his potential as an individual and as a person.

Daniel was a Jew. It is probable that he was born in Jerusalem. He came from a noble family, possibly even the royal line. At an early age, some say 14 years, he was carried as a captive to Babylon. Conditions in this pagan, sensual, idolatrous city doubtless constituted a great moral hazard to this impressionable, adolescent boy, far from his family and homeland.

Nebuchadnezzar, ruler of the Babylonian empire, had

conquered Judah and taken Jerusalem. Daniel and other carefully screened young men were carried to Babylon in order to train them for government service. Other than Daniel, the best known among these young men were the "three Hebrew children," who are remembered by their Babylonian names: Shadrach, Meshach, and Abed-nego.

Nebuchadnezzar gave the following order concerning the selection of these young men:

> *Bring certain of the children of Israel, and of the king's seed, and of the princes; children in whom is no blemish, but well favoured, and skilful in all wisdom, and cunning in knowledge, and understanding science, and such as have ability in them to stand in the king's palace, and whom they might teach the learning and the tongue of the Chaldeans* (Dan. 1:3-4).

This royal order makes it clear that these young men constituted a very select group. The entrance examinations into the King's College were rigorous and comprehensive. Only the most capable young men could "make the grade."

After admission, the students undertook a three-year course of study. It involved the languages, skills, and customs of the many and varied peoples and cultures of the vast and complex Babylonian empire. Secular history indicates that among the subjects which the young men probably studied were mathematics, astronomy, astrology, surveying, business law, comparative religions, political science, and law.

King's College of Babylon was a boarding school. Board, room, and tuition were provided at the royal expense. Like students today in similar schools, it wasn't long before Daniel and his friends complained about the food—but not because of its quality or quantity. Their objections had a moral and religious as well as a hygienic basis. Not only did they feel that the rich foods and wines were not ideal from the standpoint of health, but the meats had probably been offered to idols before being served to the students.

In any event, after a period of trial on a simple, vegetable diet, Daniel and his friends "appeared fairer and fatter in flesh than all the children which did eat the portion of the king's meat." So apparently all of the students got the new health food! At least Daniel and his friends did.

Daniel and his Hebrew companions studied hard and long. They also prayed earnestly about their studies. The result was that "God gave them knowledge and skill in all learning and wisdom." In addition, Daniel did unusually well in his clinical psychology! He was given special "understanding in all visions and dreams." This skill in dream interpretation was to be of significant value to both him and his adopted country on more than one future occasion.

After three years of diligent study, faithful discipline in their personal lives, and steadfast loyalty to the faith of their fathers, the four captive students were confronted with their final examination. It was a comprehensive, oral examination—a genuine power test! And it was given by none other than Nebuchadnezzar himself!

After conferring at length with Daniel and his friends, the king gave them grades of 90 to 100 on a scale of 0 to 100! But the next best student in the class obtained a score of not more than 10 (Dan. 1:20)! In fact, Daniel and his three friends excelled even the members of the King's College Alumni Association in their skill, knowledge, and understanding!

Not long after his graduation from King's College, Daniel interpreted a disturbing dream of Nebuchadnezzar. As a result of this remarkable service, Daniel was quickly promoted to a position of great power and influence in the Babylonian government. "Then the king made Daniel a great man, and gave him many great gifts, and made him ruler over the whole province of Babylon, and chief of the governors over all the wise men of Babylon" (Dan. 2:48).

This was but the beginning of an illustrious career. Daniel served in numerous positions of great authority and wide influence. He held the position of prime minister under four, and possibly five, different emperors. He may have actively continued in governmental service beyond his ninetieth birthday. His life was rich, full, useful, and devout.

Many years ago, the late Dr. James B. Chapman gave a commencement address entitled "The Measure of Life." He suggested that life had five dimensions and that each dimension had a specific criterion or yardstick by which it could be measured. Using Dr. Chapman's outline, let us evaluate Daniel's life.

The first dimension of life is *length*. Daniel lived a long time in terms of years. He entered King's College in his early teens. During his career he held major governmental offices under Nebuchadnezzar and Belshazzar, rulers of the Babylonian empire. He also served under Darius, the Median; and Cyrus, the Persian. Yes, Daniel lived and served God and his adopted country for many years.

In order for most of us to live very much we will need to live as many years as possible. Too often the shortening of one's life is simply a testimony to poor habits of eating, sleeping, or working. It is positively Christian, and good sense too, to give proper and consistent attention to physical health and the consequent extension of one's years of usefulness.

But years alone, and optimum health which makes possible the extension of those years, is hardly the measure of the true "length" of life. Our blessed Lord had a public ministry of only three and one-half years. But what a *long* life He lived in terms of deeds of mercy and kindness and outgoing love! Why was it long? Because He filled each day so full of deeds of practical, helpful service. We do not know all the details, but we may be sure that Daniel's days were full of such deeds, in both his personal and his public life. He was busy with affairs of state, but he also found time to serve his fellow countrymen in exile and plan for their restoration to their native land.

128

Life has another dimension: *breadth*. Someone has observed: "Life is as broad as our intellectual interests." Daniel lived a broad life by this measure. We have already seen something of his liberal education in the King's College. This had been preceded by the excellent and rigorous moral and spiritual training of the Jewish boy back in the homeland. Doubtless Daniel kept alive his intellectual interests through his long and active life. He read about the peoples and customs of many cultures and lands, and traveled extensively throughout the empire. He continued his interests in government and law, in business and in science. Only a man who was "alive at the top," and constantly growing in knowledge and understanding, could have served so many emperors with such rare distinction. Daniel had many and growing intellectual interests. He lived a broad life.

And so should we as followers of our Lord. It is said that Oliver Goldsmith was once near the end of a very long line of persons offering toasts to the king of England. When his turn came, Goldsmith said, "Good King, my toast to you is the hope that you will stay alive all the days of your life." Exactly! That is what we all need, and must have if our lives are to have the dimension of breadth.

A third dimension of life is *depth*. The true measure of the depth of life is found in a person's genuine, God-given convictions. It is customary in this day of existential philosophy to hear that modern man is suffering from his rootlessness, and the meaninglessness of his existence. Some scholars believe that the widespread lack of significance and purpose in the lives of many persons has contributed in large measure to serious personality problems. And one great authority claimed that his adult patients did not recover their mental and emotional health until and unless they recaptured a fundamental meaning in their lives.

Some deep, personal convictions about life and its

129

meaning, which give purpose and direction to life here and hope for life hereafter, have always been essential to great living. Life is as deep as our God-given convictions.

It is evident that Daniel measures up well here. He lived a deep life. To "dare to be a Daniel" has meaning for every informed child in Sunday school who has sung that song. Let us look at three of his convictions which might well be ours if we are to live "not somehow, but triumphantly."

The first was: *I will not defile my body.* As a teen-age boy, far from home and family influences, in a pagan, wicked city and in a court noted for its debauchery and drunkenness, Daniel took his stand. He purposed in his heart that he would not defile himself with the king's food or wine.

The meats which were served, as previously noted, had probably first been offered in sacrifice to idols; or perhaps they were types of meat, such as pork, which were forbidden by the Law of Moses. The wines which flowed so freely were but preludes to the bacchanalian orgies which often marked the sensuality of court life. Amid such influences, Daniel had a conviction: *I will keep my body clean and pure.* The story indicates that he took his stand firmly but with tact and good judgment, so as not to endanger the position of his friend, Malzar, the prince of the eunuchs (Dan. 1:9-16).

Daniel had another conviction: *I will consider every talent a sacred trust.* He was naturally a gifted man. In addition, God endowed him with special aptitudes, particularly in the interpretation of visions and dreams. This special talent was of unusual importance in the king's court, as was indicated in the chapter on Nebuchadnezzar. The Babylonians placed great dependence for the direction of public policy upon the advice of magicians, soothsayers, astrologers, and interpreters of visions and dreams.

But when Daniel interpreted dreams, he always gave

130

glory to God. "There is a God in heaven that revealeth secrets," he said. For Daniel, every personal gift, every talent was a sacred trust from God. He was but a steward. This was a conviction with him, and a measure of the depth of his life.

Daniel had still another bedrock conviction which gave the indispensable quality of directedness to his life: *I will not deny my God.*

Probably no story in the Bible is better known than the one about his experience in the den of lions. Darius, the Median emperor, had set 120 princes over his empire. Over these, he appointed three presidents, of whom Daniel was the first. Daniel, we are told, "was preferred above the presidents and princes, because an excellent spirit was in him; and the king thought to set him over the whole realm" (Dan. 6:3). Daniel was about to be the man above the presidents!

The presidents and princes were beside themselves with envy and jealousy. And the only place where they thought Daniel might be vulnerable was at the point of his devotional life—his worship of God. What a commentary on his skill and faithfulness as the top administrator of the empire! So the jealous officials subtly intrigued Darius into signing a degree that throughout the empire only he should be worshipped for 30 days! The penalty for noncooperation: being cast into the den of lions!

The edict did not phase Daniel. He went on with his usual three-times-daily prayer times and, what is more, with his windows open for all to hear (Dan. 6:10). No more thrilling example of personal conviction is to be found in either sacred or secular literature! Daniel would not deny his God, though the refusal might cost him his life!

Over the years from boyhood, Daniel had cultivated daily, systematic habits of prayer and devotion, and as he got older, the more like himself he became! Even though the decree was signed, he opened his window toward Jerusalem, the City of God, and prayed out loud "as he did aforetime"!

Daniel's life had *depth* as measured by his convictions concerning the purity of his body, the stewardship of every God-given talent, and his fidelity to the true and living God, who heard and answered prayer. Our lives are as deep as our convictions about the issues which matter most and which will endure forever!

Life has not only length and breadth and depth. It also has *width*. Life is as wide as our sympathies. Students of personality (who often love big words!) frequently speak of "sympathy through empathy." By this they mean that genuine sympathy is based on the ability of one person to actually enter into another person's thinking, feeling, and perceiving. True sympathy is love in action. To some extent, it involves seeing through another person's eyes, hearing through his ears, thinking through his mind, feeling through his heart. It involves responding to another person's needs, even though these may be unexpressed in words. Sympathy is one of the ways in which genuine love reveals itself in action. It is love made practical and helpful. And it is one of the great secrets of true happiness.

Daniel lived a wide life. His sympathies were as wide as the scope of his acquaintances. They included his fellow officers of administration, the varied peoples of his adopted country, and his own people in exile. As he saw the time approaching when his countrymen were to be restored to their homeland, he carried their concerns to the throne of God in prayer, and to the throne of Babylon in person.

There is a final dimension to life, and that is *height*. How shall we measure the height of a person's life? Consider this: "Life is as high as our aspirations." We do not know all the aspirations which gave the dimension of height to the life of Daniel, but they did include a supreme desire to be loyal to and serve the God of his fathers. We may be sure also that he sought to be an able and worthy

132

administrator in his adopted land as well as an instrument in the providential restoration of his people to their homeland.

When we come into the New Testament and listen to the Apostle Paul, the supreme aspiration of a follower of the Lord Jesus Christ comes into clear focus. The apostle wrote:

> But what things were gain to me, those I counted loss for Christ. Yea doubtless, and I count all things but loss for the excellency of the knowledge of Christ Jesus my Lord: for whom I have suffered the loss of all things, and do count them but dung, that I may win Christ, and be found in him, not having mine own righteousness, which is of the law, but that which is through the faith of Christ, the righteousness which is of God by faith: that I may know him, and the power of his resurrection, and the fellowship of his sufferings, being made conformable unto his death . . . this one thing I do, forgetting those things which are behind, and reaching forth unto those things which are before, I press toward the mark for the prize of the high calling of God in Christ Jesus (Phil. 3:7-10, 13-14).

For the Christian, life's highest aspiration is to have a personal knowledge of the Lord Jesus Christ, to be increasingly transfigured into the moral and spiritual likeness of his Lord (II Cor. 3:18), and to be deeply and dynamically identified with Christ in the building of His kingdom. Since life is as high as our aspirations, the result is to experience life at its highest level of personal enrichment and fulfillment.

No doubt Daniel had many imperfections. Like you and me, he was probably disappointed with himself on many occasions. But as we look back and evaluate his character and life, it seems clear that in large measure he lived fully and significantly in each of life's five dimensions:

Length—in terms of a lifetime of worthy, unselfish deeds of practical helpfulness.

133

Breadth—in terms of many continued and growing intellectual interests.

Depth—in terms of God-given convictions concerning purity of body and mind, the stewardship of every God-given talent, and ultimate and supreme loyalty to the true and living God of his fathers.

Width—in terms of his varied, active, and genuine sympathies.

Height—in terms of his lofty spiritual aspirations.

With the unerring Word of God as our Guide, the vicarious atoning death of the Lord Jesus Christ as our merit, the power of His Holy Spirit as our dynamic, and the prospect of being transfigured into the image of our Lord as our goal, let us, too, seek to attain the fullest measure of life in each of its five dimensions.

15

CALEB:
On Growing Old Successfully

Amiel, an astute observer of life, has written, "How to grow old is the master work of wisdom, and one of the most difficult chapters in the great art of living." Within certain evident limits, men age in terms of their expectations. What they tend to believe to be true *is* true, for them. Thomas Hard, who died at the age of 47, wrote, "When he is forsaken, withered and forsaken, what can an old man do but die?"

The limits within which one's expectations must operate include facing and accepting with realism and courage the inescapable physical, social, and other limitations which come with age. Yet a person's mental attitude is of crucial importance. A man is biologically as old as the elasticity of his arteries; but psychologically, he is as old as his adaptability, his flexible inner strength.

135

Age is a quality of mind:
If you have left your dreams behind,
  If hope is cold,
If you no longer look ahead,
If your ambition fires are dead,
  Then you are old.

But if from life you take the best,
And if in life you keep the jest,
  If love you hold,
No matter how the years go by,
No matter how your birthdays fly,
  You are not old.

The life of Caleb can teach us much about the art of growing old successfully. This man, who wholly followed the Lord, was full of vigor and a spirit of adventure at the age of 85. He was optimistic about the future. A difficult task still challenged him. His future was still ahead of him. Note his words: "I am this day four score and five years old. As yet I am as strong this day as I was in the day that Moses sent me: as my strength was then, even so is my strength now, for war, both to go out, and to come in. Now therefore give me this mountain" (Josh. 14:10-12).

On two different occasions, 45 years apart, Caleb played an important role in the history of the children of Israel. Both incidents occurred during the era when God's chosen people were making their way from Egyptian bondage and establishing their homes in the land of Canaan.

The first incident involved the sending of 12 "spies" to survey the Promised Land. Caleb was selected to represent the tribe of Judah on this ancient exploratory trip. Under the leadership of Moses, the people had come to Kadesh-barnea, on the southern edge of Canaan. Immediate entrance was now possible. Moses urged decisive action. "Behold," he said, "the Lord thy God hath set the land before thee: go up and possess it, as the Lord God of thy fathers hath said unto thee; fear not, neither be discouraged" (Deut. 1:21).

The people responded by suggesting that a group of representative leaders be sent to search out the land and bring word as to the best strategy for its conquest. As a result, a leading man was selected from each of the 12 tribes to make up the team. Each man was a "ruler." Only two of them are commonly remembered: Caleb, of Judah; and Joshua, who represented the tribe of Ephraim.

The mandate given to the "spies" was clear and pointed: "See the land, what it is; and the people that dwelleth therein, whether they be strong or weak, few or many; and what the land is that they dwell in, whether it be good or bad . . . and bring of the fruit of the land" (Num. 13: 18-20).

The spies were thus commissioned to take an honest, realistic look at the land, its people, and its resources. They were to add up the assets, and assess the liabilities. Both the possibilities and difficulties of conquest were to be carefully appraised.

The spies diligently followed their orders and spent 40 days in a careful study of Canaan. They traversed the land from south to north and east to west. They observed the inhabitants, and their military defenses and capabilities. Upon their return, they displayed a sample of the fruit of the land. Two men, perhaps Caleb and Joshua, carried an enormous cluster of grapes from the rich and productive Valley of Eshcol. Then came the reports of the investigators. A large majority, 10 of the 12, had this to say:

> We came unto the land whither thou sentest us, and surely it floweth with milk and honey; and this is the fruit of it. Nevertheless the people be strong that dwell in the land, and the cities are walled, and very great . . . We be not able to go up against the people; for they are stronger than we. . . . The land, through which we have gone to search it, is a land that eateth up the inhabitants thereof; and all the people that we saw in it are men of

a great stature. And there we saw the giants, the sons of Anak, which come of the giants: and we were in our own sight as grasshoppers, and so we were in their sight (Num. 13:27-33).

The reaction of the children of Israel to this seemingly hopeless and discouraging report was predictable. They lifted up their voices and wept. Murmuring against Moses and Aaron, the resentful multitude gave expression to familiar death wishes: "Would God that we had died in the land of Egypt! or would God we had died in this wilderness!" (Num. 14:2)

Caleb and Joshua were dismayed and endeavored, without success, to persuade the people to adopt an attitude and program of conquest based on faith in themselves and in God. "The land," they urged, "which we passed through to search it, is an exceeding good land. If the Lord delight in us, then he will bring us into this land, and give it us; a land which floweth with milk and honey. Only rebel ye not against the Lord, neither fear ye the people of the land; for . . . the Lord is with us: fear them not" (Num. 14:7-9).

Despite the efforts of Caleb and Joshua, the will of the fearful and unbelieving majority prevailed. The people shared their "grasshopper" perception of themselves and their resources. The Lord was exceedingly displeased. Had it not been for the intercession of Moses, the people might well have been forthrightly destroyed because of their evil hearts of unbelief. However, they were permitted to live, but the penalty for their faithlessness was severe. Of all those age 21 and upward, only Caleb and Joshua would be permitted to enter the Promised Land.

So ended the first significant episode in the life of Caleb, a man who "wholly followed the Lord." He was then in the prime of life—40 years of age.

The second great event of Caleb's life came 45 years later, following many years of wilderness wandering while

138

a whole generation of people with "grasshopper" complexes lived out their lives of futility and frustration.

The conquest of Canaan was now well under way under the vigorous and capable leadership of Joshua, who had replaced Moses. In fact, the time had come to assign certain parts of the Promised Land to the various tribes, clans, and families. Caleb came forward to remind Joshua of what Moses had said to him 45 years before: "Surely the land whereon thy feet have trodden shall be thine inheritance, and thy children's for ever" (Josh. 14:9). Of this Joshua was well aware and without hesitation assigned him the area of Hebron, in the south.

So Caleb, at 85 years of age, undertook the difficult and challenging task of conquering the hill country whose inhabitants were the giant sons of Anak. To enlist the support of his people, astute Caleb offered the hand of his attractive daughter, Achsah, in marriage to the one who would lead in the conquest of the stronghold, Kirjathsepher.

Caleb's nephew, Othniel, a "chip off the old block," accepted the challenge with something of the adventurous spirit of his uncle. The result: Othniel won the fortress, married Caleb's daughter, and received an unusually generous dowry from his proud and grateful father-in-law.

Thus Caleb, a man of faith and courage, who "wholly followed the Lord," passes from the sacred record. He was a remarkable man for his or any other day. Why was it that he towered above so many other men whose careers are recorded in the Word of God? What can we learn from his life and example?

Of fundamental importance was his perception of God, of himself, and of the problems of life. He was an idealistic-realist, or a realistic-idealist. All of that group of 12 spies went throughout Canaan with their eyes wide open. Objectively, Caleb saw exactly what the 10 fainthearted, unbelieving spies saw: a productive land of "milk and honey"; luscious and abundant fruit; great, walled cities; and fierce, gargantuan men like the sons of Anak, which came of giants.

But there is something about perception which must never be forgotten. In addition to the objective "world" of "facts as they are," there is the subjective "world" of individual interpretation. Here the "view" of Caleb and Joshua differed sharply from that of their 10 fellow spies. The latter's perception was: "We were in our own sight as grasshoppers, and so we were in their sight." The conclusion which they reached was logically related to their perception of themselves and the enemy: "We be not able to go up against the people; for they are stronger than we." Their "grasshopper" appraisal of themselves and their resources was readily shared by their enemies, who themselves feared the advancing Israelitish horde. Their reaction reveals that a person's self-image is of critical importance in determining his behavior, as well as his total outlook on life.

The anxiety-ridden majority and the courageous, believing minority were confronted with the same objective facts. But what a difference there was in their *perceptions* of these facts! Subsequent events, in fact, proved that Caleb and Joshua were accurate in their appraisal of the mental attitude of the Canaanites. Later when spies were sent by Joshua into the city of Jericho, Rahab, the harlot, reported to them, "I know that the Lord hath given you the land, and that your terror is fallen upon us, and that all the inhabitants of the land faint because of you."

The faithless, timid spies made three errors in their perception of the land of Canaan, its inhabitants, and the possibility of conquest. They *overestimated* the strength of the "giant" enemy; they *underestimated* their own strength, looking upon themselves as grasshoppers; and *they did not really believe* that the miracle-working God who had delivered them at the Red Sea and preserved them

140

in the wilderness would continue to be their Bulwark and Defense in the days ahead. Their theme song was, "We Are Not Able." They illustrated the statement, "Whether you think you can or cannot, you are right!" It seems unbelievable but probable that many of the inhabitants of Canaan had more faith in the wonder-working power of the God of Israel than did five-sixths of Israel's leading men!

In contrast to the perception of the fainthearted, Caleb gave a large and prominent place to the supernatural resources promised by the God of Abraham, Isaac, and Jacob. He had invisible means of support. The giants who had dominated the perception of the unbelieving majority faded into the background. The assurance of God's unfailing presence and power was in the forefront of Caleb's view of the situation. He had something of the divine point of view.

This divine perspective is essential to winsome, radiant, creative Christian living. The Apostle Paul prayed that "you may see things, as it were, from His [God's] point of view by being given spiritual insight and understanding" (Col. 1:9, paraphrased).

The importance of such an attitude and perspective in meeting practical problems of life is aptly illustrated by the experience of the prophet Elisha as recorded in the sixth chapter of II Kings. The prophet and his youthful assistant were surrounded in the city of Dothan by an enemy army. When the young man looked at the situation from the city wall, all he could see was the overwhelming force of the enemy. They dominated his perception, filling the foreground. Then Elisha prayed that God would touch the eyes of the servant. What a change! Now he could "see" the overwhelming spiritual resources of Almighty God which were available for their deliverance.

Caleb had such God-touched vision. He was still a realist; he saw the giants. But he also saw with the eyes of faith the overwhelming power of a great God. Little wonder, then, that he came to the unshakable conclusion: "If the Lord delight in us, then he will bring us into the land, and give it us."

Caleb was noteworthy not only for his *spiritual perception*, but for his *excellent spirit*. Like Daniel, Caleb was preferred above others by the "excellent spirit [that] was in him." God himself commended Caleb by noting that he had "another spirit"—in contrast to that of the unbelieving spies.

Caleb's "other spirit" was actually a fusion of a *living faith* in God, a *daring venturesomeness* which moved him to appropriate action, and an *optimistic outlook* toward the future.

Caleb's faith in God was no mere intellectual belief. It led him to insist upon immediate action regarding the conquest of Canaan: "Let us go up at once, and possess it; for we are well able to overcome it." The ultimate test of a vital, living faith is action. It involves acting as if the resources of Deity are available—now!

Caleb's excellent spirit also was made up of a daring courage in the face of recognized and calculated danger. He was not naive or foolhardy. He was well aware of the giants in Canaan, the walled cities, and the mountain strongholds.

One might expect a spirit of courageous adventure in a man of 40. But what about an old man of 85? Don't all men tend to rest on their achievements, and become more cautious and conservative as they grow older? Yes, most do. But not Caleb! "Give me," he said, "this mountain area inhabited by giants!" He was as daring, as venturesome, as courageous as he had been 45 years before. His request speaks volumes about his inspiring courage. And remember, "One man with courage is a majority!"

Caleb's excellent spirit was also evidenced by his orientation toward the future. He was *prospective* rather than *retrospective* in his attitude toward life. There is a subtle and almost universal tendency for men to look backward rather than forward as they grow older. The reason is that many do not actually believe they have a worthwhile future. Consequently, their consciousness tends to flow back to a time when life was fluid and open with possibilities. They tend, then, to glorify the past, the "good old days." They develop "the old-oaken-bucket delusion."

But should such regressive habits ever characterize a loyal follower of God, and especially a New Testament, born-again Christian? For such a person, isn't tomorrow always better than today? No matter how old a Christian may be, his future is still ahead of him. God's tomorrow is sure to be better than today. What a joy it is to fellowship with such older Christians—those who, like Caleb, maintain a vital, growing faith in God, in the triumph of His kingdom, and in people, including youth! Like the Apostle Paul, they are ever pressing forward to the "prize of the high calling of God in Christ Jesus" (Phil. 3:14).

Caleb was a man of unusual spiritual perceptivity, with an excellent spirit marked by a faith which led to appropriate action, an attitude of venturous daring, and a wholesome orientation toward the future. But there is still one additional factor which accounts for his remarkable life. It is this: *He wholly followed the Lord.* At age 85 his testimony was, "I wholly followed the Lord my God" (Josh. 14:8). Even more important, God himself declared, "But my servant Caleb, because he had another spirit with him, and *hath followed me fully*, him will I bring into the land whereinto he went" (Num. 14:24, italics mine).

Caleb, like the Apostle Paul, was a man of singleness of purpose in following the Lord. Like Paul, he could have testified, "This *one* thing I do." Consequently, his life had focus and power.

There is a Promised Land of spiritual enrichment and creative service which our Lord has promised to all who will wholly follow Him. The challenge to you and me today, as to Caleb long ago, is to "go up at once, and possess it."

Caleb did indeed possess his inheritance. His "success formula" may well become a model for you and me in the arena of spiritual conflict and conquest. Is it too much to hope that you and I, should we reach the age of 85, will have the daring faith to request of God: "Give me this mountain"? And let us never forget that God is able "to do exceeding abundantly above all that we ask or think, according to the power that worketh in us" (Eph. 3:20).